GALIT SHMUELI

KENNETH C. LICHTENDAHL JR.

PRACTICAL TIME SERIES FORECASTING WITH R

A HANDS-ON GUIDE

AXELROD SCHNALL PUBLISHERS

PUBLISHED BY AXELROD SCHNALL PUBLISHERS

ISBN-13: 978-0-9915766-3-0

ISBN-10: 0991576632

Cover art: Drying coconuts (copra), Kerala, India. Copyright © 2015 Boaz Shmueli

For further information see www.forecastingbook.com

First Edition, July 2015

Contents

4

To Boaz Shmueli, who made the production

of this book series a reality

Preface

The purpose of this textbook is to introduce the reader to quantitative forecasting of time series in a practical and hands-on fashion. From our experience, learning is best achieved by doing. Hence, the book is designed to achieve self-learning in the following ways:

- The book is relatively short compared to other time series textbooks, to reduce reading time and increase hands-on time.

- Explanations strive to be clear and straightforward with more emphasis on concepts than on theory.

- Chapters include end-of-chapter problems, ranging in their focus from conceptual to hands-on exercises, with many requiring running software on real data and interpreting the output in light of a given problem.

- Real data are used to illustrate the methods throughout the book.

- The book emphasizes the *entire forecasting process* rather than focusing only on particular models and algorithms.

- Cases are given in the last chapter, guiding the reader through suggested steps, but allowing self-solution. Working on the cases should help integrate the information and experience gained.

Course Plan

The book is designed for a 6-7 week forecasting course at the graduate or upper-undergraduate level. A suggested schedule is:

Week 1   Chapters 1 ("Approaching Forecasting") and 2 ("Data") cover goal definition; data collection, characterization, visualization, and pre-processing.

Week 2   Chapter 3 ("Performance Evaluation") covers data partitioning, naive forecasts, measuring predictive accuracy and uncertainty.

Weeks 3-4   Chapter 4 ("Forecasting Methods: Overview") describes and compares different approaches underlying forecasting methods. Chapter 5 ("Smoothing Methods") offers a smooth entry to popular forecasting methods. It covers moving average, exponential smoothing, and differencing.

Week 5   Chapter 6 ("Regression-Based Models") covers linear regression models, second-level models, autocorrelation and ARIMA models.

Week 6   Chapter 8 ("Communication and Maintenance") discusses practical issues of presenting, reporting, documenting and monitoring forecasts. This week is a good point for providing feedback on a case analysis from Chapter 9.

Week 7 (optional)   Chapter 7 ("Other Forecasting Methods") discusses the inclusion of external information and forecasting binary outcomes. In introduces the methods of logistic regression and neural networks.

A team project is highly recommended in such a course, where students work on a real or realistic problem using real data.

Software and Data

The free and open-source software *R* (www.r-project.org) is used throughout the book to illustrate the different methods and procedures. This choice is good for students who are comfortable with some computing language, but does not require prior knowledge with R. We provide code for figures and outputs to help readers easily replicate our results while learning the basics of R. In particular, we use the R *forecast package*, (`robjhyndman.com/software/forecast`) which provides computationally efficient and user-friendly implementations of many forecasting algorithms.

To create a user-friendly environment for using R, download both the R software from `www.r-project.org` and RStudio from `www.rstudio.com`.

Finally, we advocate using interactive visualization software for exploring the nature of the data before attempting any modeling, especially when many series are involved. Two such packages are Tableau (`www.tableausoftware.com`) and TIBCO Spotfire (`spotfire.tibco.com`). We illustrate the power of these packages in Chapter 1, and the book website provides two interactive dashboards for experiencing the power of interactive exploration of time series.

Datasets used in the chapter exercises and examples and in the cases are publicly available at `www.forecastingbook.com`.

Acknowledgments

Many thanks to Professor Rob Hyndman (Monash University) for inspiring this edition and providing invaluable information about the R "forecast" package. Thanks to Professor Ravi Bapna and Peter Bruce for their useful feedback and suggestions. Special thanks to Noa Shmueli for her meticulous editing.

1
Approaching Forecasting

In this first chapter, we look at forecasting within the larger context of where it is implemented and introduce the complete forecasting process. We also briefly touch upon the main issues and approaches that are detailed in the book.

1.1 Forecasting: Where?

Time series forecasting is performed in nearly every organization that works with quantifiable data. Retail stores forecast sales. Energy companies forecast reserves, production, demand, and prices. Educational institutions forecast enrollment. Governments forecast tax receipts and spending. International financial organizations such as the World Bank and International Monetary Fund forecast inflation and economic activity. Passenger transport companies use time series to forecast future travel. Banks and lending institutions forecast new home purchases, and venture capital firms forecast market potential to evaluate business plans.

1.2 Basic Notation

The amount of notation in the book is kept to the necessary minimum. Let us introduce the basic notation used in the book. In particular, we use four types of symbols to denote time periods, data series, forecasts, and forecast errors:

$t = 1, 2, 3, \ldots$ An index denoting the time period of interest. $t = 1$ is the first period in a series.

$y_1, y_2, y_3, \ldots, y_n$ A series of n values measured over n time periods, where y_t denotes the value of the series at time period t. For example, for a series of daily average temperatures, $t = 1, 2, 3, \ldots$ denotes day 1, day 2, and day 3; $y_1, y_2,$ and y_3 denote the temperatures on days 1,2, and 3.

F_t The forecasted value for time period t.

F_{t+k} The k-step-ahead forecast when the forecasting time is t. If we are currently at time period t, the forecast for the next time period ($t + 1$) is denoted F_{t+1}.

e_t The forecast error for time period t, which is the difference between the actual value and the forecast at time t, and equal to $y_t - F_t$ (see Chapter 3).

1.3   The Forecasting Process

As in all data analysis, the process of forecasting begins with *goal definition*. Data are then collected and cleaned, and explored using visualization tools. A set of potential forecasting methods is selected, based on the nature of the data. The different methods are applied and compared in terms of forecast accuracy and other measures related to the goal. The "best" method is then chosen and used to generate forecasts.

Of course, the process does not end once forecasts are generated, because forecasting is typically an ongoing goal. Hence, forecast accuracy is monitored and sometimes the forecasting method is adapted or changed to accommodate changes in the goal or the data over time. A diagram of the forecasting process is shown in Figure 1.1.

Note the two sets of arrows, indicating that parts of the process are iterative. For instance, once the series is explored one might determine that the series at hand cannot achieve the required goal, leading to the collection of new or supplementary data. Another iterative process takes place when applying a forecasting method and evaluating its performance. The evaluation often leads to tweaking or adapting the method, or even trying out other methods.

Figure 1.1: Diagram of the forecasting process

Given the sequence of steps in the forecasting process and the iterative nature of modeling and evaluating performance, the book is organized according to the following logic: In this chapter we consider the context-related goal definition step. Chapter 2 discusses the steps of data collection, exploration, and pre-processing. Next comes Chapter 3 on performance evaluation. The performance evaluation chapter precedes the forecasting method chapters for two reasons:

1. Understanding how performance is evaluated affects the choice of forecasting method, as well as the particular details of how a particular forecasting method is executed. Within each of the forecasting method chapters, we in fact refer to evaluation metrics and compare different configurations using such metrics.

2. A crucial initial step for allowing the evaluation of predictive performance is data partitioning. This means that the forecasting method is applied only to a subset of the series. It is therefore important to understand why and how partitioning is carried out before applying any forecasting method.

The forecasting methods chapters (Chapters 5, 6, and 7) are followed by a chapter on "Implementing Forecasts" (Chapter 8), which discusses the last step of implementing the forecasts or forecasting system within the organization.

Before continuing, let us present an example that will be used throughout the book for illustrative purposes.

Illustrative Example: Ridership on Amtrak Trains

Amtrak, a U.S. railway company, routinely collects data on ridership. Our illustration is based on the series of monthly Amtrak ridership between January 1991 and March 2004 in the United States.

The data are publicly available at www.forecastingprinciples. com (click on *Data*, and select Series M-34 from the T-Competition Data) as well as on the book website.

Figure 1.2: (Image by graur codrin / FreeDigitalPhotos.net)

1.4   Goal Definition

Determining and clearly defining the forecasting goal is essential for arriving at useful results. Unlike typical forecasting competitions[1], where a set of data with a brief story and a given set of performance metrics are provided, in real life neither of these components are straightforward or readily available. One must first determine the purpose of generating forecasts, the type of forecasts that are needed, how the forecasts will be used by the organization, what are the costs associated with forecast errors, what data will be available in the future, and more.

It is also critical to understand the *implications* of the forecasts to different stakeholders. For example, The National Agricultural Statistics Service (NASS) of the United States Department of Agriculture (USDA) produces forecasts for different crop yields. These forecasts have important implications:

> [S]ome market participants continue to express the belief that the USDA has a hidden agenda associated with producing the estimates and forecasts [for corn and soybean yield]. This "agenda" centers on price manipulation for a variety of purposes, including such things as managing farm program costs and influencing food prices. Lack of understanding of NASS methodology and/or the belief in a hidden agenda can prevent market participants from correctly interpreting and utilizing the acreage and yield forecasts.[2]

In the following we elaborate on a few important issues that must be considered at the goal definition stage. These issues affect every step in the forecasting step, from data collection through data exploration, preprocessing, modeling and performance evaluation.

Descriptive vs. Predictive Goals

As with cross-sectional data[3], modeling time series data is done for either descriptive or predictive purposes. In descriptive modeling, or *time series analysis*, a time series is modeled to determine its components in terms of seasonal patterns, trends, relation to external factors, and the like. These can then be used for decision making and policy formulation. In contrast, *time series forecasting*

[1] For a list of popular forecasting competitions see the "Data Resources and Competitions" pages at the end of the book

[2] From farmdocdaily blog, posted March 23, 2011, www.farmdocdaily.illinois.edu/2011/03/post.html; accessed Dec 5, 2011.

[3] Cross-sectional data are a set of measurements taken at one point in time. In contrast, a time series consists of one measurement over time.

uses the information in a time series (perhaps with additional information) to forecast future values of that series. The difference between descriptive and predictive goals leads to differences in the types of methods used and in the modeling process itself. For example, in selecting a method for describing a time series or even for explaining its patterns, priority is given to methods that produce explainable results (rather than black-box methods) and to models based on causal arguments. Furthermore, description can be done in retrospect, while prediction is prospective in nature. This means that descriptive models can use "future" information (e.g., averaging the values of yesterday, today, and tomorrow to obtain a smooth representation of today's value) whereas forecasting models cannot. Finally, a predictive model is judged by its predictive accuracy rather than by its ability to provide correct causal explanations.

Consider the Amtrak ridership example described at the beginning of this chapter. Different analysis goals can be specified, each leading to a different path in terms of modeling, performance evaluation, and implementation. One possible analysis goal that Amtrak might have is to forecast future monthly ridership on its trains for purposes of pricing. Using demand data to determine pricing is called "revenue management" and is popular practice by airlines and hotel chains. Clearly, this is a predictive goal.

A different goal that Amtrak might want to use the ridership data is for evaluating the effect of some event, such as airport closures due to inclement weather, or the opening of a new large national highway. This goal is retrospective in nature, and is therefore descriptive or even explanatory. Analysis would compare the series before and after the event, with no direct interest in future values of the series. Note that these goals are also geography-specific and would therefore require using ridership data at a finer level of geography within the United States.

A third goal that Amtrak might pursue is identifying and quantifying demand during different seasons for planning the number and frequency of trains needed during different seasons. If the model is only aimed at producing monthly indexes of demand, then it is a descriptive goal. In contrast, if the model will be used to forecast seasonal demand for future years, then it is a predictive task.

Finally, the Amtrak ridership data might be used by national agencies, such as the Bureau of Transportation Statistics, to evaluate the trends in transportation modes over the years. Whether this is a descriptive or predictive goal depends on what the analysis will be used for. If it is for the purposes of reporting past trends, then it is descriptive. If the purpose is forecasting future trends, then it is a predictive goal.

The focus in this book is on *time series forecasting*, where the goal is to predict future values of a time series. Some of the methods presented, however, can also be used for descriptive purposes.[4]

[4] Most statistical time series books focus on descriptive *time series analysis*. A good introduction is the book .
  C. Chatfield. *The Analysis of Time Series: An Introduction.* Chapman & Hall/CRC, 6th edition, 2003

Forecast Horizon and Forecast Updating

How far into the future should we forecast? Must we generate all forecasts at a single time point, or can forecasts be generated on an ongoing basis? These are an important questions to be answered at the goal definition stage. Both questions depend on how the forecasts will be used in practice and therefore require close collaboration with the forecast stakeholders in the organization. The forecast horizon k is the number of periods ahead that we must forecast, and F_{t+k} is a k-step-ahead forecast. In the Amtrak ridership example, one-month-ahead forecasts (F_{t+1}) might be sufficient for revenue management (for creating flexible pricing), whereas longer term forecasts, such as three-month-ahead (F_{t+3}), are more likely to be needed for scheduling and procurement purposes.

How recent are the data available at the time of prediction? Timeliness of data collection and transfer directly affect the forecast horizon: Forecasting next month's ridership is much harder if we do not yet have data for the last two months. It means that we must generate forecasts of the form F_{t+3} rather than F_{t+1}. Whether improving timeliness of data collection and transfer is possible or not, its implication on forecasting must be recognized at the goal definition stage.

While long-term forecasting is often a necessity, it is important to have realistic expectations regarding forecast accuracy: the farther into the future, the more likely that the forecasting context will change and therefore uncertainty increases. In such cases, expected changes in the forecasting context should be incorporated into the forecasting model, and the model should be examined periodically to assure its suitability for the changed context and if possible, updated.

Even when long-term forecasts are required, it is sometimes useful to provide periodic updated forecasts by incorporating new accumulated information. For example, a three-month-ahead forecast for April 2012, which is generated in January 2012, might be updated in February and even March of the same year.

All these aspects of the forecast horizon have implications on the required length of the series for building the forecast model, on frequency and timeliness of collection, on the forecasting methods used, on performance evaluation, and on the uncertainty levels of the forecasts.

Forecast Use

How will the forecasts be used? Understanding how the forecast will be used, perhaps by different stakeholders, is critical for generating forecasts of the right type and with a useful accuracy level. Should forecasts be numerical or binary ("event"/"non-event")? Does over-prediction cost more or less than under-prediction? Will the forecasts be used directly or will they be "adjusted" in some way before use? Will the forecasts and forecasting method to be presented to management or to the technical department? The answers to such questions is necessary for choosing appropriate data, methods, and evaluation schemes.

Level of Automation

The level of required automation depends on the nature of the forecasting task and on how forecasts will be used in practice. Some important questions to ask are:

1. How many series need to be forecasted?

2. Is the forecasting a continuing process or a one time event?

3. Which data and software will be available during the forecasting period?

4. What forecasting expertise will be available at the organization during the forecasting period?

Different answers will lead to different choices of data, forecasting methods, and evaluation schemes. Hence, these questions must be considered already at the goal definition stage.

In scenarios where many series are to be forecasted on a continuous basis, and not much forecasting expertise can be allocated to the process, an automated solution can be advantageous. A classic example is forecasting Point of Sale (POS) data for purposes of inventory control across many stores. Various consulting firms offer automated forecasting systems for such applications.

1.5   Problems

Impact of September 11 on Air Travel in the United States: The Research and Innovative Technology Administration's Bureau of Transportation Statistics (BTS) conducted a study to evaluate the impact of the September 11, 2001, terrorist attack on U.S. transportation. The study report and the data can be found at `www.bts.gov/publications/estimated_impacts_of_9_11_on_us_travel`. The goal of the study was stated as follows:

> The purpose of this study is to provide a greater understanding of the passenger travel behavior patterns of persons making long distance trips before and after September 11.

Figure 1.3: (Image by africa / FreeDigitalPhotos.net)

The report analyzes monthly passenger movement data between January 1990 and April 2004. Data on three monthly time series are given in the file *Sept11Travel.xls* for this period: (1) actual airline revenue passenger miles (Air), (2) rail passenger miles (Rail), and (3) vehicle miles traveled (Auto).

In order to assess the impact of September 11, BTS took the following approach: Using data before September 11, it forecasted future data (under the assumption of no terrorist attack). Then, BTS compared the forecasted series with the actual data to assess the impact of the event.

1. Is the goal of this study descriptive or predictive?

2. What is the forecast horizon to consider in this task? Are next-month forecasts sufficient?

3. What level of automation does this forecasting task require? Consider the four questions related to automation.

4. What is the meaning of $t = 1, 2, 3$ in the Air series? Which period does $t = 1$ refer to?

5. What are the values for y_1, y_2, and y_3 in the Air series?

2

Data

2.1 Data Collection

When considering which data to use for generating forecasts, the forecasting goal and the various aspects discussed in Chapter 1 must be taken into account. There are also considerations at the data level which can greatly affect the forecasting results. Next, we will look at several such issues.

Data Quality

The quality of our data in terms of measurement accuracy, missing values, corrupted data and data entry errors can greatly affect the forecasting results. Data quality is especially important in time series forecasting, where the sample size is very small (typically not more than a few hundred values in a series).

If there are multiple sources collecting or hosting the data of interest (e.g., different departments in an organization), it can be useful to compare the quality and choose the best data (or even combine the sources!). However, it is important to keep in mind that for ongoing forecasting, data collection is not a one-time effort. Additional data will need to be collected again in future from the same source. Moreover, if forecasted values will be compared against a particular series of actual values, then that series must play a major role in the performance evaluation step. For example, if forecasted daily temperatures will be compared against measurements from a particular weather station, forecasts based on measurements from other sources should be compared to the data from that weather station.

In some cases the series of interest alone is sufficient for arriving at satisfactory forecasts, while in other cases external data might be more predictive of the series of interest than solely its history. In the case of external data, it is crucial to assure that the same data will be available at the time of prediction.

Temporal Frequency

With today's technology, many time series are recorded on very frequent time scales. Stock ticker data are available on a minute-by-minute level. Purchases at online and brick and mortar stores are recorded in real time. However, although data might be available at a very frequent scale, for the purpose of forecasting it is not always preferable to use this frequency. In considering the choice of temporal frequency, one must consider the frequency of the required forecasts (that is, the goal) and the level of noise[1] in the data. For example, if the goal is to forecast next-day sales at a grocery store, minute-by-minute sales data are likely less useful than daily aggregates. The minute-by-minute series will contain many sources of noise (e.g., variation by peak and nonpeak shopping hours) that degrade its daily-level forecasting power, yet when the data are aggregated to a coarser level, these noise sources are likely to cancel out.

Even when forecasts are needed on a particular frequency (such as daily) it is sometimes advantageous to aggregate the series to a lower frequency (such as weekly), and model the aggregated series to produce forecasts. The aggregated forecasts can then be disaggregated to produce higher-frequency forecasts. For example, the top performers in the 2008 *NN5 Time Series Forecasting Competition*[2] describe their approach for forecasting daily cash withdrawal amounts at ATM machines:

> To simplify the forecasting problem, we performed a time aggregation step to convert the time series from daily to weekly...Once the forecast has been produced, we convert the weekly forecast to a daily one by a simple linear interpolation scheme.

[1] "Noise" refers to variability in the series' values that is not to account for. See Section 2.2.

[2] R. R. Andrawis, A. F. Atiya, and H. El-Shishiny. Forecast combinations of computational intelligence and linear models for the NN5 time series forecasting competition. *International Journal of Forecasting*, 27:672–688, 2011

Series Granularity

"Granularity" refers to the coverage of the data. This can be in terms of geographical area, population, time of operation, etc. In the Amtrak ridership example, depending on the goal we could look at geographical coverage (route-level, state-level, etc.), at a particular type of population (e.g., senior citizens), and/or at particular times (e.g., during rush hour). In all these cases, the resulting time series are based on a smaller population of interest than the national level time series.

As with temporal frequency, the level of granularity must be aligned with the forecasting goal, as well as consider levels of noise. Very fine coverage might lead to low counts, perhaps even to many zero counts. Exploring different aggregation and slicing levels is often needed for obtaining adequate series. The level of granularity will eventually affect the choice of preprocessing, forecasting method(s), and evaluation metrics. For example, if we are interested in daily train ridership of senior citizens on a particular route, and the resulting series contains many zero counts, we might resort to methods for forecasting binary data rather than numeric data (see Chapter 7).

Domain Expertise

While the focus in this section is on the quantitative data to be used for forecasting, a critical additional source of information is domain expertise. Without domain expertise, the process of creating a forecasting model and evaluating its usefulness is unlikely to achieve its goal.

Domain expertise is needed for determining which data to use (e.g., daily vs. hourly, how far back, and from which source), describing and interpreting patterns that appear in the data, from seasonal patterns to extreme values and drastic changes (e.g., clarifying what are "after hours", interpreting massive absences due to the organization's annual picnic, and explaining the drastic change in trend due to a change in company policy).

Domain expertise is also used for helping evaluate the practical implications of the forecasting performance. As we discuss in Chapter 8, implementing the forecasts and the forecasting system requires close linkage with the organizational goals. Hence, the ability to communicate with domain experts during the forecasting process is crucial for producing useful results, especially when the forecasting task is outsourced to a consulting firm.

2.2   *Time Series Components*

For the purpose of choosing adequate forecasting methods, it is useful to dissect a time series into a systematic part and a non-systematic part. The systematic part is typically divided into three components: *level*, *trend*, and *seasonality*. The non-systematic part is called *noise*. The systematic components are assumed to be unobservable, as they characterize the underlying series, which we only observe with added noise. *Level* describes the average value of the series, *trend* is the change in the series from one period to the next, and *seasonality* describes a short-term cyclical behavior that can be observed several times within the given series. While some series do not contain trend or seasonality, all series have a level. Lastly, *noise* is the random variation that results from measurement error or other causes not accounted for. It is always present in a time series to some degree, although we cannot observe it directly.

The different components are commonly considered to be either *additive* or *multiplicative*. A time series with *additive* components can be written as:

$$y_t = \text{Level} + \text{Trend} + \text{Seasonality} + \text{Noise} \qquad (2.1)$$

A time series with *multiplicative* components can be written as:

$$y_t = \text{Level} \times \text{Trend} \times \text{Seasonality} \times \text{Noise} \qquad (2.2)$$

Forecasting methods attempt to isolate the systematic part and quantify the noise level. The systematic part is used for generating point forecasts and the level of noise helps assess the uncertainty associated with the point forecasts.

Trend patterns are commonly approximated by linear, exponential and other mathematical functions. Illustrations of different trend patterns can be seen by comparing the different rows in Figure 2.1. For seasonal patterns, two common approximations are *additive seasonality* (where values in different seasons vary by a constant amount) and *multiplicative seasonality* (where values in different seasons vary by a percentage). Illustrations of these seasonality patterns are shown in the second and third columns of Figure 2.1. Chapter 6 discusses these different patterns in further detail, and also introduces another systematic component, which is the correlation between neighboring values in a series.

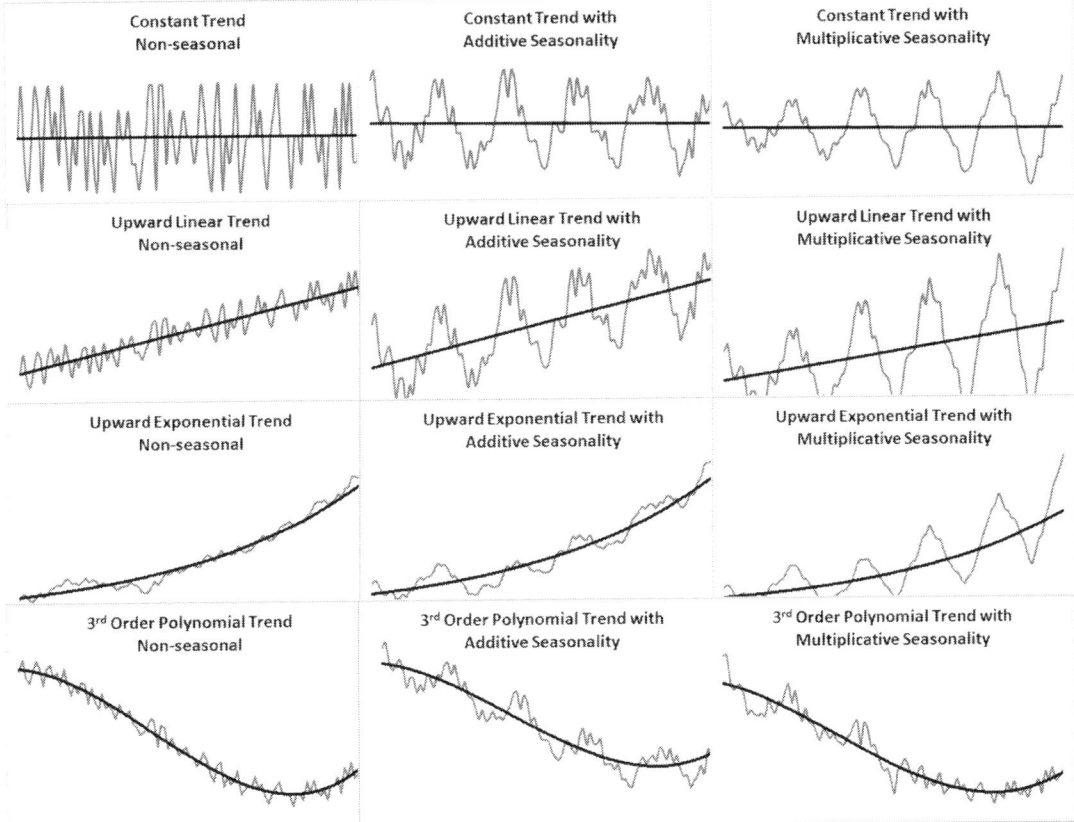

Figure 2.1: Illustrations of common trend and seasonality patterns. Reproduced with permission from Dr. Jim Flower's website jcflowers1.iweb.bsu.edu/rlo/trends.htm

2.3 Visualizing Time Series

An effective initial step for characterizing the nature of a time
series and for detecting potential problems is to use data visualization. By visualizing the series we can detect initial patterns,
identify its components and spot potential problems such as
extreme values, unequal spacing, and missing values.

The most basic and informative plot for visualizing a time
series is the *time plot*. In its simplest form, a time plot is a line
chart of the series values $(y_1, y_2, \ldots)$ over time $(t = 1, 2, \ldots)$, with
temporal labels (e.g., calendar date) on the horizontal axis. To
illustrate this, consider the Amtrak ridership example. A time
plot for monthly Amtrak ridership series is shown in Figure
2.3. Note that the values are in thousands of riders. Looking
at the time plot reveals the nature of the series components:
the overall level is around 1,800,000 passengers per month. A
slight U-shaped trend is discernible during this period, with
pronounced annual seasonality; peak travel occurs during the
summer months of July and August.

A second step in visualizing a time series is to examine it
more carefully. The following operations are useful:

Zooming in: Zooming in to a shorter period within the series can reveal patterns that are hidden when viewing the entire series. This is especially important when the time series is
long. Consider a series of the daily number of vehicles passing
through the Baregg tunnel in Switzerland[3] (data are available in
the same location as the Amtrak ridership data; series D028). The
series from November 1, 2003 to November 16, 2005 is shown
in the top panel of Figure 2.5. Zooming in to a 4-month period
(bottom panel) reveals a strong day-of-week pattern that was not
visible in the initial time plot of the complete time series.

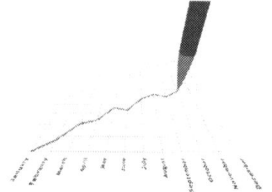

Figure 2.2: Line plot. (Image by Danilo Rizzuti /
FreeDigitalPhotos.net)

[3] The Baregg tunnel, between
Bern and Zurich, is one
of the busiest stretches of
motorways in Switzerland.

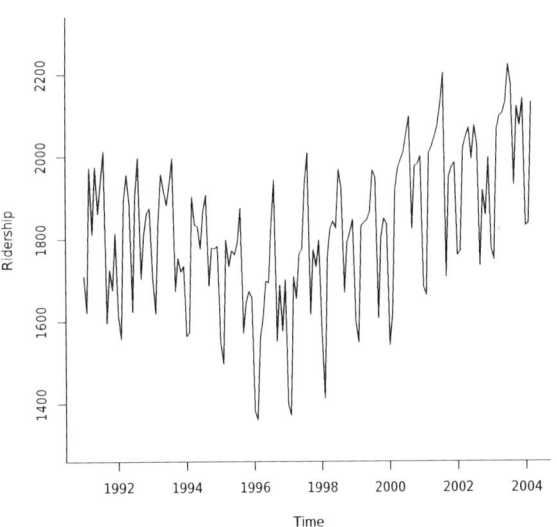

Figure 2.3: Monthly ridership on Amtrak trains (in
thousands) from Jan-1991 to
March-2004

 code for creating Figure 2.3.

```
Amtrak.data <- read.csv("Amtrak data.csv")
ridership.ts <- ts(Amtrak.data$Ridership, start = c(1991,1), end = c(2004, 3), freq = 12)
plot(ridership.ts, xlab = "Time", ylab = "Ridership", ylim = c(1300, 2300), bty = "l")
```

To create a user-friendly environment for using R, download both the R software from
www.r-project.org and RStudio from www.rstudio.com. Before running the code above
in RStudio, save the Amtrak data in Excel as a csv file called Amtrak data.csv. The first
line reads the csv file into the data frame called Amtrak.data. The function ts creates a
time series object out of the data frame's first column Amtrak.data$Ridership. We give the
time series the name ridership.ts. This time series starts in January 1991, ends in March
2004, and has a frequency of 12 months per year. By defining its frequency as 12, we can
later use other functions to examine its seasonal pattern. The third line above produces the
actual plot of the time series. R gives us control over the labels, axes limits, and the plot's
border type.

Figure 2.4: Baregg Tunnel, Switzerland. Source: Wikimedia Commons

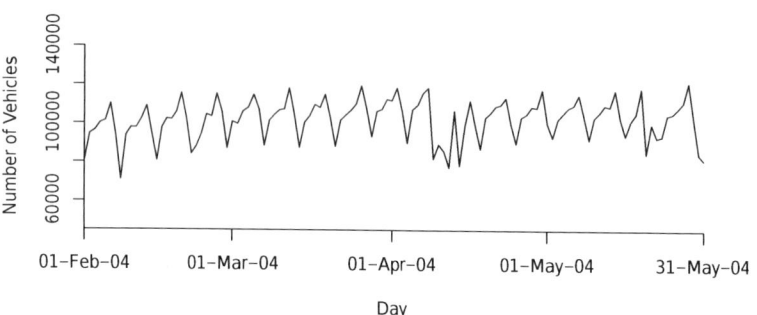

Figure 2.5: Time plots of the daily number of vehicles passing through the Baregg tunnel. The bottom panel zooms in to a 4-month period, revealing a day-of-week pattern.

Changing the Scale: In order to better identify the shape of a trend, it is useful to change the scale of the series. One simple option is to change the vertical scale (of y) to a logarithmic scale. (In Excel 2003 double-click on the y-axis labels and check "logarithmic scale"; in Excel 2007 select *Layout > Axes > Primary Vertical Axis* and click "logarithmic scale" in the *Format Axis* menu). If the trend on the new scale appears more linear, then the trend in the original series is closer to an exponential trend.

Adding Trend Lines: Another possibility for better capturing the shape of the trend is to add a trend line (Excel 2003: *Chart > Add Trendline*; Excel 2007: *Layout > Analysis > Trendline*). By trying different trend lines one can see what type of trend (e.g., linear, exponential, cubic) best approximates the data.

Suppressing Seasonality: It is often easier to see trends in the data when seasonality is suppressed. Suppressing seasonality patterns can be done by plotting the series at a cruder time scale (e.g., aggregating monthly data into years). A second option is to plot separate time plots for each season. A third popular option is to use moving average plots. We will discuss moving average plots in Section 5.2.

Continuing our example of Amtrak ridership, the plots in Figure 2.6 help make the series' components more visible. Some forecasting methods directly model these components by making assumptions about their structure. For example, a popular assumption about trend is that it is linear or exponential over parts, or all, of the given time period. Another common assumption is about the noise structure: many statistical methods assume that the noise follows a normal distribution. The advantage of methods that rely on such assumptions is that when the assumptions are reasonably met, the resulting forecasts will be more robust and the models more understandable. In contrast, data-driven forecasting methods make fewer assumptions about the structure of these components and instead try to estimate them only from the data.

Time plots are also useful for characterizing the global or local nature of the patterns. A global pattern is one that is relatively constant throughout the series. An example is a linear trend throughout the entire series. In contrast, a local pattern is one that occurs only in a short period of the data, and then changes. An example is a trend that is approximately linear within four neighboring time points, but the trend size (slope) changes slowly over time. Operations such as zooming in can help establish more subtle changes in seasonal patterns or trends across periods. Breaking down the series into multiple sub-series and overlaying them in a single plot can also help establish whether a pattern (such as weekly seasonality) changes from season to season.

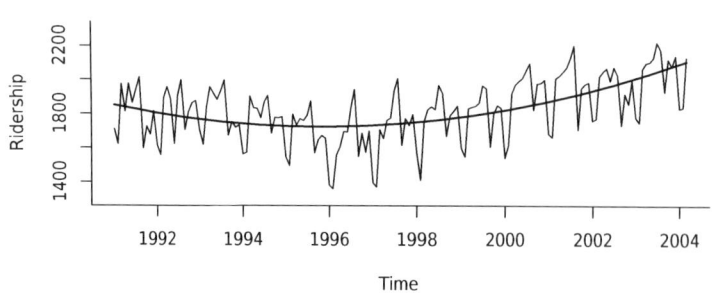

Figure 2.6: Plots that enhance the different components of the time series. Top: overlaid polynomial trend line. Bottom: original series with zoom in to 4 years of data.

 code for creating Figure 2.6

```
install.packages(forecast)
library("forecast")
ridership.lm <- tslm(ridership.ts ~ poly(trend, 2))
par(mfrow = c(2, 1))
plot(ridership.ts, xlab = "Time", ylab = "Ridership", ylim = c(1300, 2300), bty = "l")
lines(ridership.lm$fitted, lwd = 2)
ridership.ts.zoom <- window(ridership.ts, start = c(1997, 1), end = c(2000, 12))
plot(ridership.ts.zoom, xlab = "Time", ylab = "Ridership", ylim = c(1300, 2300), bty = "l")
```

Install the package forecast and load the package with the function library. To fit a quadratic trend, run the forecast package's linear regression model for time series, called tslm. The y variable is ridership, and the two x variables are trend $= (1, 2, \ldots, 159)$ and the square of trend. Plot the time series and its fitted regression line in the top panel of Figure 2.6. The bottom panel shows a zoomed in view of the time series from January 1997 to December 2000. Use the window function to identify a subset of a time series.

2.4   Interactive Visualization

The various operations described above: zooming in, changing scales, adding trendlines, aggregating temporally, breaking down the series into multiple time plots, are all possible using software such as Excel. However, each operation requires generating a new plot or at least going through several steps until the modified chart is achieved. The time lag between manipulating the chart and viewing the results detracts from our ability to compare and "connect the dots" between the different visualizations. Interactive visualization software offer the same functionality (and usually much more), but with the added benefit of very quick and easy chart manipulation. An additional powerful feature of interactive software is the ability to link multiple plots of the same data. Operations in one plot, such as zooming in, will then automatically also be applied to all the linked plots. A set of such linked charts is often called a "dashboard".

Figure 2.7 shows a screenshot of an interactive dashboard built for the daily Baregg tunnel traffic data. The dashboard is publicly available on the book website and at `public.tableausoftware.com/views/BareggTunnelTraffic/Dashboard`. To best appreciate the power of interactivity, we recommend that you access this URL, which allows direct interaction with the visualization.

The top panel displays an ordinary time plot (as in the top panel of Figure 2.5). Just below the date axis is a zoom slider, which can be used to zoom-in to specific date ranges. The zoom slider was set to be "global" so that when applied, all charts in the dashboard are affected.

Recall that aggregating the data by looking at more coarse temporal frequencies can help suppress seasonality. The second panel shows the same data, this time aggregated by month. In addition, a quadratic trendline is fitted separate to each year. To break down the months into days, click on the plus sign at the bottom left of the panel (the plus sign appears when you hover over the Monthly Average panel). Note that the daily view will display daily data and fit separate quadratic trends to each month.

Another visualization approach to suppressing seasonality

is to look separately at each season. The bottom panel in the dashboard uses separate lines for different days of week. The filter on the right allows the user to display only lines for certain days and not for others (this filter was set to affect only the bottom panel). It is now clear what the fluctuations in the top panel were indicating: tunnel traffic differs quite significantly between different days of week, and especially between Sundays (the lowest line) and other days. This information might lead us to forecast Sunday traffic separately.

Figure 2.8 shows another example of how interactive dashboards are useful for exploring time series data. This dashboard includes time plots for three related series: monthly passenger movement data on air, rail, and vehicles in the United States between 1990-2004. These data are introduced in the problems of Chapter 6. Looking at the three series, aligned horizontally, highlights the similar seasonal pattern that they share. The filters on the right allow zooming in for each series separately. The slider below the x-axis at the bottom allows zooming in to particular date ranges. This will affect all series. Additionally, we can aggregate the data to another temporal level by using the small "Date(Month)" slider at the very bottom. In this example, we can look at yearly, quarterly and monthly sums. Looking at annual numbers suppresses the monthly seasonal pattern, thereby magnifying the long-term trend in each of the series (ignore year 2004, which only has data until April).

The slider to the left of the y-axis allows zooming in to a particular range of values of the series. Note that each series has a different scale on the y-axis, but that the filter will still affect all of the series.

The filters and sliders in the right panel again can be used for zooming in temporally or in terms of the series values. The "Date" allows looking at particular years or quarters. For instance, we can remove year 2001, which is anomalous (due to the September 11 terror attack). Lastly, we can choose a particular part of a series by clicking and dragging the mouse. The data for the observations that fall in the chosen area will then be presented in the bottom-right "Details-on-Demand" panel.

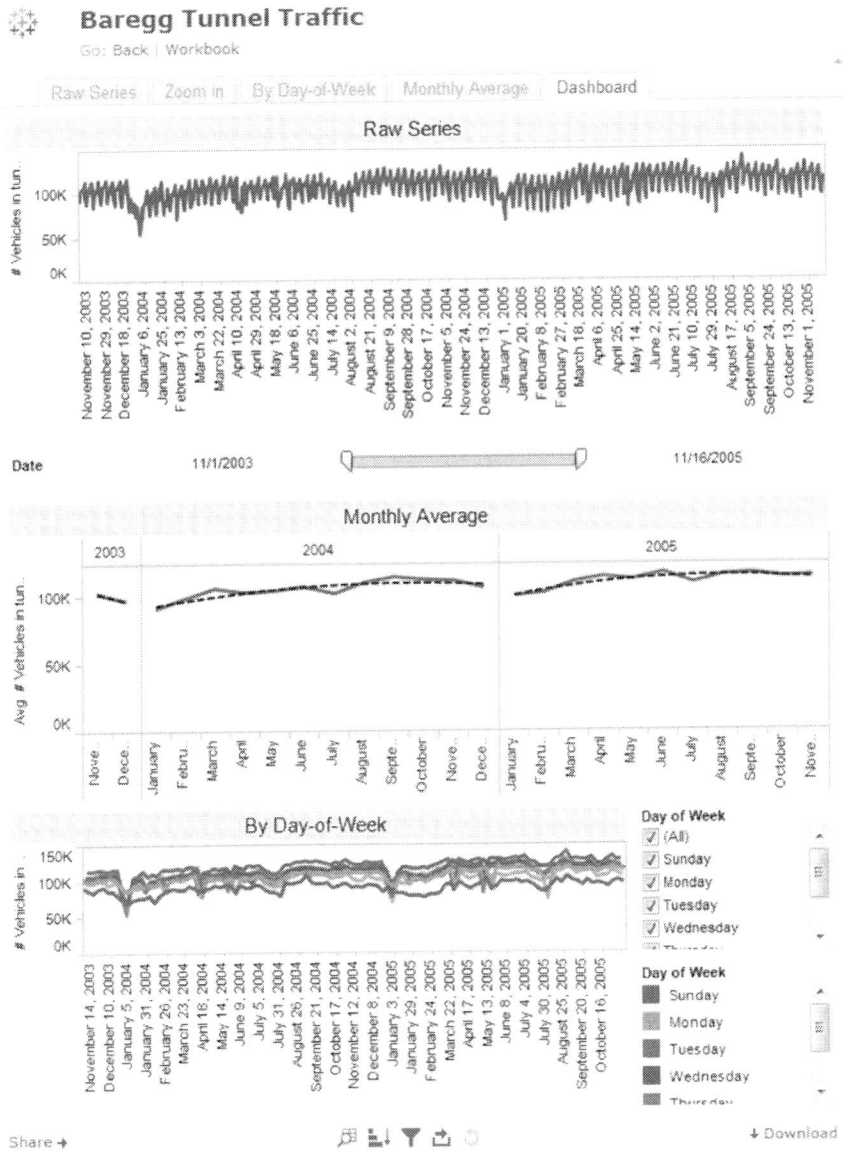

Figure 2.7: Screenshot of an interactive dashboard for visualizing the Baregg tunnel traffic data. The dashboard, created using the free Tableau Public software, is available for interaction at www.forecastingbook.com.

Figure 2.8: Screenshot of an interactive dashboard for visualizing the September 11, 2001 passenger movement data. The dashboard, created using TIBCO Spotfire software, is available for interaction at www.forecastingbook.com.

2.5   Data Pre-Processing

If done properly, data exploration can help detect problems such as possible data entry errors as well as missing values, unequal spacing and irrelevant periods. In addition to addressing such issues, pre-processing the data also includes a preparation step for enabling performance evaluation, namely data partitioning. We discuss each of these operations in detail next.

Missing Values

Missing values in a time series create "holes" in the series. The presence of missing values has different implications and requires different actions depending on the forecasting method. Forecasting methods such as ARIMA models and smoothing methods (in Chapters 6 and 5) cannot be directly applied to time series with missing values, because the relationship between consecutive periods is modeled directly. With such methods, it is also impossible to forecast values that are beyond a missing value if the missing value is needed for computing the forecast. In such cases, a solution is to impute, or "fill in", the missing values. Imputation approaches range from simple solutions, such as averaging neighboring values, to creating forecasts of missing values using earlier values or external data.

In contrast, forecasting methods such as linear and logistic regression models and neural networks (Sections 6.1-6.3 and Chapter 7), can be fit to a series with "holes", and no imputation is required. The implication of missing values in such cases is that the model/method is fitted to less data points. Of course, it is possible to impute the missing values in this case as well. The tradeoff between data imputation and ignoring missing values with such methods, is the reliance on noisy imputation (values plus imputation error) vs. the loss of data points for fitting the forecasting method. One could, of course, take an ensemble approach where both approaches, one based on imputed data and the other on dropped missing values, are implemented and the two are combined for forecasting.

Missing values can also affect the ability to generate forecasts and to evaluate predictive performance (see Section 3.1).

In short, since some forecasting methods cannot tolerate missing values in a series and others can, it is important to discover any missing values before the modeling stage.

Unequally Spaced Series

An issue related to missing value is unequally spaced data. Equal spacing means that the time interval between two consecutive periods is equal (e.g., daily, monthly, quarterly data). However, some series are naturally unequally spaced. These include series that measure some quantity during events where event occurrences are random (such as bus arrival times), naturally unequally spaced (such as holidays or music concerts), or determined by someone other than the data collector (e.g., bid timings in an online auction).

As with missing values, some forecasting methods can be applied directly to series that are unequally spaced, while others cannot. Converting an unequally spaced series into an equally spaced series typically involves interpolation using approaches similar to those for handling missing values.

Extreme Values

Extreme values are values that are unusually large or small compared to other values in the series. Extreme value can affect different forecasting methods to various degrees. The decision whether to remove an extreme value or not must rely on information beyond the data. Is the extreme value the result of a data entry error? Was it due to an unusual event (such as an earthquake) that is unlikely to occur again in the forecast horizon? If there is no grounded justification to remove or replace the extreme value, then the best practice is to generate two sets of forecasts: those based on the series with the extreme values and those based on the series excluding the extreme values.

Choice of Time Span

Another pre-processing operation that is sometimes required is determining how far back into the past should be considered. In other words, what is the time span of the data to be used. While a very short (and recent) series might be insufficiently informative for forecasting purposes, the addition of historical data beyond a certain duration will likely be useless at best, and harmful at worst. Considering a very long history of the series might deteriorate the accuracy of future forecasts because of the changing context and environment. For example, in many countries transportation demand for flights by traditional airlines drastically changed when low-cost airlines entered the market. Using data that spans from both periods to forecast future demand on traditional carriers is therefore adding disruptive information. A particular example is first class ridership on Indian Railways.[4] When low-cost airlines entered the domestic Indian market in the early 2000s, first-class ridership on trains plunged in favor of air travel. A few years later, the first-class rail fares were substantially reduced, and first class train ridership levels have since increased. Hence, the length of the series for forecasting first-class demand on Indian Railways must extend backwards only to periods where the environment is assumed to be similar to the forecast horizon.

[4] http://knowindia.net/rail.html

2.6 Problems

1. *Impact of September 11 on Air Travel in the United States:* The Research and Innovative Technology Administration's Bureau of Transportation Statistics (BTS) conducted a study to evaluate the impact of the September 11, 2001, terrorist attack on U.S. transportation. The study report and the data can be found at `www.bts.gov/publications/estimated_impacts_of_9_11_on_us_travel`. The goal of the study was stated as follows:

   > The purpose of this study is to provide a greater understanding of the passenger travel behavior patterns of persons making long distance trips before and after September 11.

   The report analyzes monthly passenger movement data between January 1990 and April 2004. Data on three monthly time series are given in the file *Sept11Travel.xls* for this period: (1) actual airline revenue passenger miles (Air), (2) rail passenger miles (Rail), and (3) vehicle miles traveled (Auto).

   In order to assess the impact of September 11, BTS took the following approach: Using data before September 11, it forecasted future data (under the assumption of no terrorist attack). Then, BTS compared the forecasted series with the actual data to assess the impact of the event.

   Plot each of the three pre-event time series (Air, Rail, Car).

   (a) What time series components appear from the plot?

   (b) What type of trend appears? Change the scale of the series, add trend lines, and suppress seasonality to better visualize the trend pattern

2. *Forecasting Department Store Sales:* The file *DepartmentStore-Sales.xls* contains data on the quarterly sales for a department store over a 6-year period (data courtesy of Chris Albright).

   (a) Create a well-formatted time plot of the data.

   (b) Which of the four components (level, trend, seasonality, noise) seem to be present in this series?

Figure 2.9: Air travel. (Image by africa / FreeDigitalPhotos.net)

Figure 2.10: (Image by Paul Martin Eldridge / FreeDigitalPhotos.net)

3. *Shipments of Household Appliances:* The file *ApplianceShipments.xls* contains the series of quarterly shipments (in million USD) of U.S. household appliances between 1985 and 1989 (data courtesy of Ken Black).

   (a) Create a well-formatted time plot of the data.

   (b) Which of the four components (level, trend, seasonality, noise) seem to be present in this series?

4. *Analysis of Canadian Manufacturing Workers Work-Hours:* The time series plot below describes the average annual number of weekly hours spent by Canadian manufacturing workers (data available in *CanadianWorkHours.xls*, courtesy of Ken Black).

   (a) Reproduce the time plot.

   (b) Which of the four components (level, trend, seasonality, noise) appear to be present in this series?

Figure 2.11: (Image by Salvatore Vuono / FreeDigitalPhotos.net)

Figure 2.12: Average annual weekly hours spent by Canadian manufacturing workers

5. *Souvenir Sales:* The file *SouvenirSales.xls* contains monthly sales for a souvenir shop at a beach resort town in Queensland, Australia, between 1995 and 2001. [source: Hyndman, R. J.

Time Series Data Library, http://data.is/TSDLdemo; accessed on July 13, 2015.]

Back in 2001, the store wanted to use the data to forecast sales for the next 12 months (year 2002). They hired an analyst to generate forecasts. The analyst first partitioned the data into training and validation periods, with the validation period containing the last 12 months of data (year 2001). She then fit a regression model to sales, using the training period.

(a) Create a well-formatted time plot of the data.

(b) Change the scale of the x axis, of the y axis, or of both to logarithmic scale in order to achieve a linear relationship. Select the time plot that seems most linear.

(c) Comparing the two time plots, what can be said about the type of trend in the data?

Figure 2.13: Beach Resort. (Image by quyenlan / FreeDigitalPhotos.net)

6. *Forecasting Shampoo Sales:* The file *ShampooSales.xls* contains data on the monthly sales of a certain shampoo over a 3-year period. (source: Hyndman, R. J. Time Series Data Library, http://data.is/TSDLdemo; accessed on July 13, 2015.)

(a) Create a well-formatted time plot of the data.

(b) Which of the four components (level, trend, seasonality, noise) seem to be present in this series?

(c) Do you expect to see seasonality in sales of shampoo? Why?

3
Performance Evaluation

At first glance, we might think it best to choose the model that generates the best forecasts on the data series at hand. However, when we use the same data both to develop the forecasting model and to assess its performance, we introduce bias. This is because when we choose the model that works best with the data, this model's superior performance comes from two sources:

1. a superior model

2. chance aspects of the data that happen to match the chosen model better than they match other models

The latter is a particularly serious problem with techniques that do not impose linear or other structure on the data, and thus end up *overfitting* the data. Overfitting means that the model is not only fitting the systematic component of the data, but also the noise. An over-fitted model is therefore likely to perform poorly on new data. To illustrate the notion of overfitting, consider the analogy of a tailor sewing a new suit for a customer. If the suit is tailored to the customer's exact measurements, it will likely not be useful beyond immediate use, as small fluctuations in weight and body size over time are normal.

3.1 *Data Partitioning*

To address the problem of overfitting, an important preliminary step before applying any forecasting method is data partitioning, where the series is split into two periods. We develop our forecasting model or method using only one of the periods. After we have a model, we try it out on another period and see how it performs. In particular, we can measure the forecast errors, which are the differences between the predicted values and the actual values, as described in the next section.

In cross-sectional data, we typically deal with two or three data partitions: a *training set*, a *validation set*, and sometimes an additional *test set*. Partitioning the data into training, validation, and test sets is typically done randomly. The training partition, typically the largest partition, contains the data used to build the various models we are examining. The same training partition is generally used to develop multiple models. The validation partition is used to assess the performance of each model so that you can compare models and pick the best one. The test partition (sometimes called the holdout or evaluation partition) is used if we need to assess the performance of the chosen model with new data.

Temporal Partitioning

In time series forecasting, as in the case of cross-sectional data, in order to avoid overfitting and to be able to assess the predictive performance of the model on new data, we first partition the data into a *training period* and a *validation period*. However, there is one important difference between data partitioning in cross-sectional and time series data. In cross-sectional data the partitioning is usually done randomly, with a random set of observations designated as training data and the remainder as validation data. However, in time series, a random partition creates two problems: Firstly, it does not mimic the temporal uncertainty where we use the past and present to forecast the future. Secondly, it creates two time series with "holes", whereas many standard forecasting methods cannot handle time series with missing values. Therefore, time series partitioning into training and validation sets is done differently: The series is trimmed into two periods where the earlier period ($t = 1, 2, \ldots, n$) is set as the training period and the later period ($t = n + 1, n + 2, \ldots$) as the validation period. An illustration is shown in Figure 3.1. *Methods are then trained on the earlier training period, and their predictive performance assessed on the later, validation period.* In evaluating and comparing forecasting methods, time plots of the actual and predicted series during both training and validation periods can shed light on performance issues and indicate possible improvements.

Note that in time series partitioning there is typically no third *test period*, which would have comprised of the most recent periods in the series. The reason is that the omission of the most recent periods from the performance evaluation, and the omission of an even longer recent period from the training period, are likely to cause more harm than benefit.

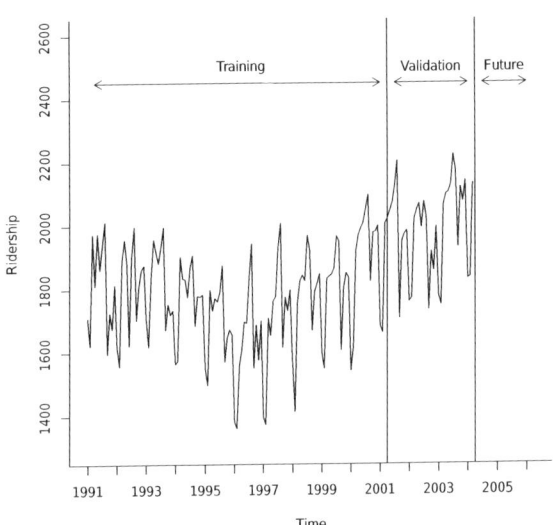

Figure 3.1: Example of temporal partitioning of the monthly ridership data. The training period is Jan 1991 to Dec 2000; the validation period is Jan 2001 to March 2004. Forecasts are required for the future period (from April 2004 onward).

Joining Partitions for Forecasting

One last important difference between cross-sectional and time series partitioning occurs when generating the actual forecasts. Before attempting to forecast future values of the series, the training and validation periods must be recombined into one long series, and the chosen method/model is rerun on the complete data. This final model is then used to forecast future values. The three advantages in recombining are:

1. The validation period, which is the most recent period, usually contains the most valuable information in terms of being the closest in time to the forecasted period.

2. With more data (the complete time series, compared to only the training period), some models can be estimated more accurately.

3. If only the training period is used to generate forecasts, then it will require forecasting farther into the future. For example, if the validation set contains four time points, forecasting the next observation will require a five-step-ahead forecast from the training set (F_{n+5}).

Figure 3.2 shows the forecasts in the validation period from a quadratic trend model applied to the Amtrak ridership training data (ignore the details of the model itself for now).

Choosing the Validation Period

The choice of the length of the validation period closely depends on the forecasting goal, on the data frequency, and on the forecast horizon. The main principle is to choose a validation period that mimics the forecast horizon, to allow evaluating actual predictive performance. For instance, in the Amtrak ridership example, if the forecasting model will be used to produce forecasts for the next year, then the validation period should include at least a year. Choosing a shorter validation period will not allow evaluating the predictive performance of longer-term forecasts. Choosing a validation period of more than a year means that our training period contains less recent information, and therefore the model based on the training period will miss out on the most recent information available at the time of prediction.

Note: The presence of missing values in the training period can affect the ability to train a forecasting method, thereby requiring

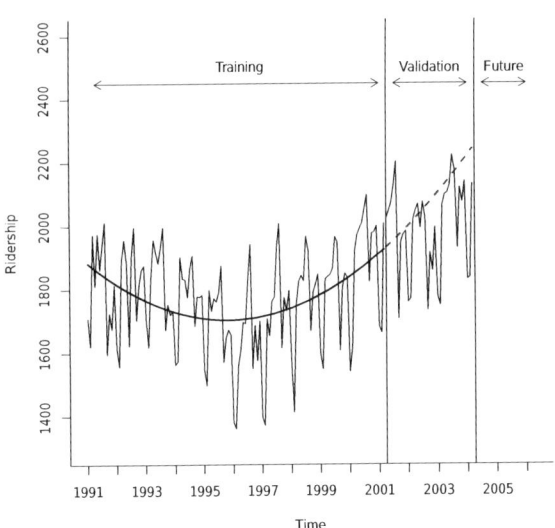

Figure 3.2: Forecasts in the validation period from a quadratic trend model estimated from the training period (Amtrak ridership data).

 code for creating Figure 3.2

```
nValid <- 36
nTrain <- length(ridership.ts) - nValid
train.ts <- window(ridership.ts, start = c(1991, 1), end = c(1991, nTrain))
ridership.lm <-  tslm(train.ts ~ poly(trend, 2))
ridership.lm.pred <- forecast(ridership.lm, h = nValid, level = 0)

plot(ridership.lm.pred, ylim = c(1300, 2600),  ylab = "Ridership", xlab = "Time", bty = "l",
    xaxt = "n", xlim = c(1991,2006.25), main = "", flty = 2)
axis(1, at = seq(1991, 2006, 1), labels = format(seq(1991, 2006, 1)))
lines(ridership.lm$fitted, lwd = 2)
lines(valid.ts)
```

Define the numbers of months in the training and validation sets, nValid and nTrain, respectively. Use the window function to create the training set. Fit a model (here a linear regression model) to the training set. Use the forecast function to make predictions of the time series in the validation period. Plot the predictions. (We omit the code for the lines and labels that demark the time partitions.)

imputation for some forecasting methods (see Section 2.5). As for a validation period with missing values, we can still evaluate predictive performance by ignoring the missing points (see Section 3.4 for details).

3.2   Naive Forecasts

Although it is tempting to apply "sophisticated" forecasting methods, one must remember to consider *naive forecasts*. A naive forecast is simply the most recent value of the series. In other words, at time t, the k-step-ahead naive forecast is given by

$$F_{t+k} = y_t \tag{3.1}$$

In the case of a seasonal series, the *seasonal naive forecast* is the value from the most recent identical season (e.g., forecast December using last December's value). For a series with M seasons, we can write the formula

$$
\begin{aligned}
F_{t+1} &= y_{t-M+1} \\
F_{t+2} &= y_{t-M+2} \\
\vdots \;&= \\
F_{t+k} &= y_{t-M+k}
\end{aligned}
\tag{3.2}
$$

The underlying logic is that the most recent information is likely to be the most relevant for forecasting the future. Naive forecasts are used for two purposes:

1. As the actual forecasts of the series. Naive forecasts, which are simple to understand and easy implement, can sometimes achieve sufficiently useful accuracy levels. Following the principle of "the simplest method that does the job", naive forecasts are a serious contender.

2. As a baseline. When evaluating the predictive performance of a certain method, it is important to compare it to some baseline. Naive forecasts should always be considered as a baseline, and the comparative advantage of any other methods considered should be clearly shown.

As with forecasts in general, the predictive performance of naive forecasts is evaluated on the validation period, and we can examine the corresponding forecast error distribution and create prediction intervals.

3.3   Measuring Predictive Accuracy

When the purpose of forecasting is to generate accurate forecasts, it is useful to define performance metrics that measure predictive accuracy. Such metrics can tell us how well a particular method performs in general, as well as compared to benchmarks or forecasts from other methods.

Let us emphasize that *predictive accuracy* (or *forecast accuracy*) is not the same as *goodness of fit* or *strength of fit*. Hence, classical measures of performance that are aimed at finding a model that fits the data well and measure the strength of relationship do not tell us about the ability of a model to accurately predict new values. In linear regression, for example, measures such as R^2 and *standard error of estimate* are popular strength of fit measures, and residual analysis is used to gauge goodness of fit where the goal is to find the best fit for the data. However, these measures do not tell us much about the ability of the model to predict new cases accurately.

For evaluating predictive performance, several measures are commonly used to assess the predictive accuracy of a forecasting method. In all cases, *the measures are based on the validation period,* which serves as a more objective basis than the training period to assess predictive accuracy (because records in the validation period are not used to select predictors or to estimate model parameters). Measures of accuracy use the prediction error that results from predicting the validation period with the model that was trained on the training period.

Common Prediction Accuracy Measures

The forecast error (or residual) for time period t, denoted e_t, is defined as the difference between the actual value (y_t) and the forecast value at time t: $e_t = y_t - F_t$. Consider a validation period with v periods. For simplicity, we will use the indexing $t = 1, \ldots, v$ instead of the more accurate but longer notation $t = n + 1, \ldots, n + v$. A few popular measures of predictive accuracy are:

MAE or MAD (mean absolute error/deviation) $= \frac{1}{v} \sum_{t=1}^{v} |e_t|$. This gives the magnitude of the average absolute error.

Average error $= \frac{1}{v} \sum_{t=1}^{v} e_t$. This measure is similar to MAD except that it retains the sign of the errors, so that negative errors cancel out positive errors of the same magnitude. It therefore gives an indication of whether the forecasts are on average over- or under-predicting.

MAPE (mean absolute percentage error) $= \frac{1}{v} \sum_{t=1}^{v} |\frac{e_t}{y_t}| \times 100\%$. This measure gives a percentage score of how forecasts deviate (on average) from the actual values. It is useful for comparing performance across series of data that have different scales.

RMSE (root mean squared error) $= \sqrt{\frac{1}{v} \sum_{t=1}^{v} e_t^2}$. This measure has the same units as the data series.

To illustrate the computation of these measures, consider Table 3.1 which shows the validation period results of applying a quadratic trend model to the Amtrak ridership data.

Month	Forecast	Actual Value	Forecast Error
Apr 2001	1932.454	2023.792	91.338
May 2001	1939.508	2047.008	107.500
Jun 2001	1946.670	2072.913	126.243
⋮	⋮	⋮	⋮
Mar 2004	2243.161	2132.446	-110.715

Table 3.1: Validation period results of applying a quadratic trend model to the Amtrak ridership data.

We use the last column (forecast errors) to compute each of the four predictive measures as follows:

$$MAE = \frac{1}{36} (|91.338| + \cdots + |-110.715|) = 133.738$$

$$Average\ error = \frac{1}{36} (91.338 + \cdots + (-110.715)) = -83.962$$

$$MAPE \;=\; \frac{1}{36}\left(\left|\frac{91.338}{2023.792}\right| + \cdots + \left|\frac{-110.715}{2132.446}\right|\right) \times 100\% = 7.076\%$$

$$RMSE \;=\; \sqrt{\frac{1}{36}\left((91.338)^2 + \cdots + (-110.715)^2\right)} = \sqrt{32345.81} = 179.849$$

 code for computing predictive measures

```
valid.ts <- window(ridership.ts, start = c(1991, nTrain + 1), end = c(1991, nTrain + nValid))
accuracy(ridership.lm.pred$mean, valid.ts)
```

Use the window function to create the valiation set. Use the accuracy function in the forecast package to calculate the four predictive measures shown above.

Note: Computing these measures using the training period does not tell us about predictive accuracy. Instead, it measures how closely the model fits the training period (goodness-of-fit).

Zero counts

When the series contains zero counts, computing MAPE results in an infinite number due to the division by y_t. One solution is to compute MAPE by excluding the zero values, which solves the technical problem but excludes information that might be important. Another solution is to use other measures such as MAE and RMSE (if appropriate). However, the appeal of MAPE as a scale-independent measure has led to the development of the scale-independent *Mean Absolute Scaled Error* (MASE) metric[1], which can handle zero counts. MASE is a scaled version of MAE, which benchmarks the model's forecast errors against the average naive forecast error by dividing the model MAE by the MAE of the naive forecasts on the training set. The reason for using the *training set* to compute the naive forecast MAE is to avoid a zero value in the denominator, which can occur due to the fewer observations in the validation period.

[1] R. J. Hyndman. Another look at forecast-accuracy metrics for intermittent demand. *Foresight: The International Journal of Applied Forecasting*, 4:43–46, 2006

$$MASE = \frac{\text{validation MAE}}{\text{training MAE of naive forecasts}} = \frac{\frac{1}{v}\sum_{t=n+1}^{n+v}|e_t|}{\frac{1}{n-1}\sum_{t=1}^{n}|y_{t-1} - y_t|}$$

$$(3.3)$$

Because MASE compares the model predictive performance (MAE) to the naive forecast on the training set, values less than 1 indicate that the model has a lower average error than naive forecasts (in the training period). Values higher than 1 indicate poor performance relative to (training period) naive forecasts.

Note that another difference between MAPE and MASE is that MAPE gives a heavier penalty to positive errors (over-forecasts) than negative errors (under-forecasts), while MASE weighs both types of errors equally.

Forecast Accuracy vs. Profitability

The popular measures of MAPE and RMSE are "pessimistic" in the sense that they give more weight to larger errors.[2] In some contexts large deviations are as bad as small deviations

In many contexts forecast accuracy is not an adequate performance measure, but rather it is combined with some costs to produce a "profitability" measure. In such cases, it is better to use the profitability measure directly in the performance evaluation step. Costs of forecast errors can be indifferent to the direction of forecast errors (positive/negative), or more sensitive to one direction. For example, under-estimating demand has different implications from over-estimating demand. Costs of forecast errors can be indifferent to the magnitude of the error beyond some threshold (e.g., if the error is larger than 5% or not), or they can be proportional to the magnitude, where "proportional" can vary from linear to very non-linear.

While we expect that overall increased predictive accuracy will lead to increased profitability, one case where the two are uncorrelated is when the process being forecasted undergoes stable and extreme periods and when costs are a function of y_t rather than e_t. An example is financial markets, where the forecasted direction of, say, a stock price would lead to a trader's decision to buy or sell at a certain price. The profitability in this case depends on the difference between the actual price (y_t) and zero, rather than on $y_t - F_t$. In such cases, forecasting methods that perform no better than random during stable periods but better than random during extreme periods will likely have

[2] MAPE is based on percentage errors and RMSE on squared errors. Both functions inflate large values relative to small values.

overall positive profitability, although they are likely to show low predictive accuracy. For a discussion and detailed example of this phenomenon see the article by Batchelor.[3]

An extreme example of a cost function that carries heavy, but different, penalties in each direction is the recent trial of six Italian scientists and a former government official over the 2009 earthquake in L'Aquilla, Italy. According to BBC News,[4]

> Prosecutors accuse the defendants gave a falsely reassuring statement before the quake after studying hundreds of tremors that had shaken the city ... The defendants face up to 15 years in jail.

Erring in the opposite direction and issuing false alarms also carries a high cost:

> Scientists could warn of a large earthquake every time a potential precursor event is observed, however this would result in huge numbers of false alarms which put a strain on public resources and might ultimately reduce the public's trust in scientists.[5]

Choosing the right profitability measure in this context is therefore dependent on *who* is measuring (the scientists or the government) and how false alerts are measured against disasters that were not forecasted.

[3] R. Batchelor. Accuracy versus profitability. *Foresight: The International Journal of Applied Forecasting*, 21:10–15, 2011

[4] BBC News Europe. Italy scientists on trial over L'aquilla earthquake, 2011. Accessed Nov 1, 2011

[5] BBC News Science & Environment. Can we predict when and where quakes will strike?, 2011. Accessed Nov 1, 2011

3.4   Evaluating Forecast Uncertainty

Distribution of Forecast Errors

Popular forecasting methods such as regression models and smoothing methods produce forecast errors that are typically not normally distributed. Forecast errors might not be independent, and not even be symmetrical around zero. While measures such as RMSE and MAPE are favorites in forecasting competitions, in practice it is important to examine not only these aggregates but the entire set of forecast errors that they comprise.

We examine the forecast errors not so much for testing for model assumptions (as in linear regression), but more to evaluate forecast uncertainty. Of interest are extremely low or high errors, reflecting extreme over- or under-forecasting. Creating a time plot and histogram of the forecast errors is also very useful. For instance, see Figures 3.3 and 3.4 for a time plot and histogram of forecast errors from a quadratic trend model applied to the Amtrak ridership data. From such plots, we can learn about the distribution of forecast errors, and the chances of obtaining forecast errors of different directions and magnitudes. Asymmetries might be useful in some contexts, where, for instance we prefer a high chance of small over-prediction but do not mind large under-predictions.

Note: When the validation period contains missing values, one can compute performance metrics such as MAE, RMSE and MAPE that exclude the missing periods. Similarly, forecast error plots can be created excluding the missing periods.

Prediction Intervals

A *prediction interval* is a forecast range, which has an uncertainty level attached to it. A prediction interval is more informative than a single forecast number (F_t), because it tells us about the risk or uncertainty associated with the forecast. For example, to forecast next month sales, the point forecast $F_t = \$50,000$ does not tell us how far the forecast can go above or below this number. In contrast, a 95% prediction interval of [\$40,000,\$52,000] tells us that we are 95% certain that the value will fall within this interval. Note that in this example the point forecast \$50,000 is not in the middle of the interval.

If forecast errors were normally distributed, prediction intervals would easily be constructed by adding/subtracting a few standard deviations to the point forecast F_t, similar to prediction intervals in cross-sectional regression analysis.[6] Figure 3.5 depicts such 95% prediction intervals from a quadratic model applied to the Amtrak ridership data.

A model's forecast errors, however, are not always normally distributed. For example, we can see from Figure 3.4 that the distribution of forecast errors (from a quadratic trend model applied to the Amtrak ridership data) does not look normal. The left tail of the histogram is longer than the right tail.[7]

When errors are not normally distributed, forecast errors can

[6] Recall that a 95% prediction interval for normally distributed errors is $F_t \pm 1.96s$, where s is the estimated standard deviation.

[7] Another quick way to check normality is using *normal probability plots,* where the forecast errors, sorted from low to high, are plotted against normal percentiles. To create a normal probability plot in R, put the forecast error into the function qqnorm.

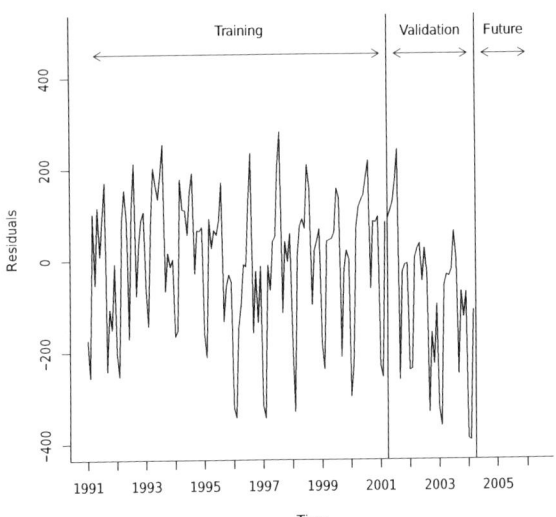

Figure 3.3: Time plot of forecast errors (or residuals) from a quadratic trend model applied to the Amtrak ridership data.

 code for calculating the residuals in Figure 3.3

```
names(ridership.lm.pred)
ridership.lm.pred$residuals
valid.ts - ridership.lm.pred$mean
```

Use the names function to find out which elements are included with the forecast object called ridership.lm.pred. The model's residuals are the forecast errors in the training period. Subtracting the model's mean (or forecasts) from valid.ts (or actuals) in the validation period gives the forecast errors in the validation period.

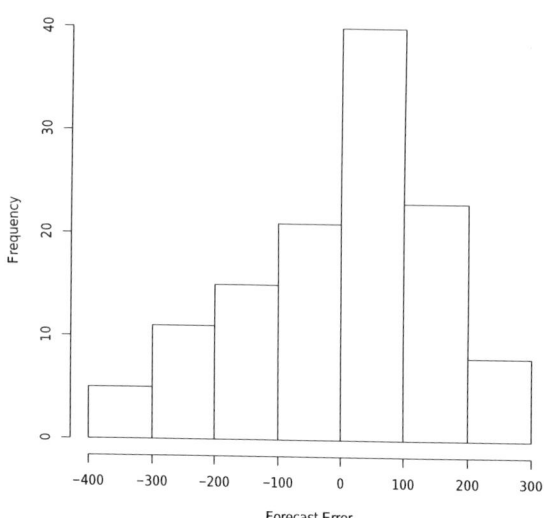

Figure 3.4: Histogram of forecast errors in the training period from a quadratic trend model applied to the Amtrak ridership data.

 code for creating the histogram in Figure 3.4

```
hist(ridership.lm.pred$residuals,  ylab = "Frequency", xlab = "Forecast Error", bty = "l", main = "")
```

Put the model's residuals into the hist function to plot the histogram, or frequency of forecast errors in each of seven (automatically and equally sized) bins.

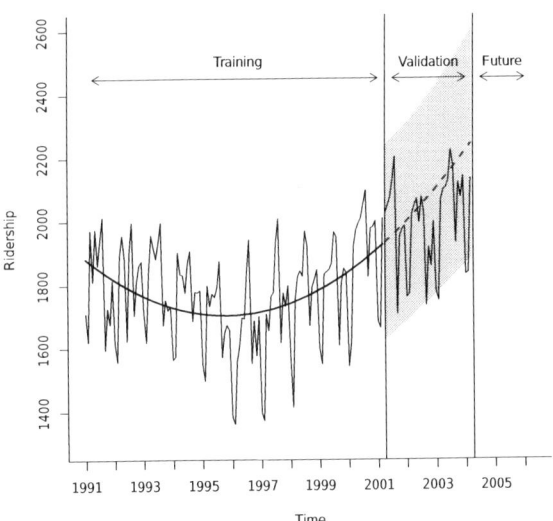

Figure 3.5: Point forecasts and 95% prediction intervals in the validation period from a quadratic trend model applied to the Amtrak ridership data. The R code for creating this plot is the same as the code used for Figure 3.2, except with `level = 95`.

be obtained from the training period to construct a prediction interval in the validation period (and future). For example, a 95% prediction interval can be constructed by using the 5th and 95th percentiles from the sample of forecast errors.[8]

[8] To compute a percentile (also known as a quantile), use R's `quantile` function.

3.5   Advanced Data Partitioning: Roll-Forward Validation

The method of partitioning the data into fixed training and validation periods presented in Section 3.1 allows us to evaluate predictive performance in a somewhat limited way: we only see a single one-step-ahead forecast, a single two-step-ahead forecast, etc. For example, if we have monthly data with three years of validation data, then we only see performance of a single one-month-ahead forecast, two-months-ahead forecast, three-month-ahead forecast, etc.

An alternative that gives us more evaluation data is to use a *roll-forward* validation period. This means creating multiple training-validation partitions by moving the partitioning one period at a time. This simulates a deployment scenario where we refresh our forecasts period-by-period. In the monthly ridership example, we can create multiple data partitions by rolling forward one month at a time, as shown in Table 3.2.

Data Partition	Training Period	Validation Period
1	Jan 1991 - Mar 2001	Apr 2001 - Mar 2004
2	Jan 1991 - Apr 2001	May 2001 - Mar 2004
3	Jan 1991 - May 2001	Jun 2001 - Mar 2004
⋮	⋮	⋮
36	Jan 1991 - Feb 2003	Mar 2004

Table 3.2: Roll-forward data partitioning (monthly updating)

The 36 partitions give us 36 one-month-ahead forecasts, 35 two-months-ahead forecasts, 34 three-months-ahead forecasts, etc. Notice that we would only have a single 36-month-ahead forecast. With roll-forward partitions, we therefore have more information about short-term forecasts, and the amount of data decreases as we move farther into future forecasting.[9]

The next step, as in fixed partitioning, is to fit a model to the training period and evaluate it on the validation period. In the roll-forward scenario this means re-running our model on each of the training sets ("refreshing" the model), and using each of the models for forecasting the corresponding validation period.

Finally, we compute performance measures using all the validation data, preferably breaking it down by one-step-ahead performance, two-step-ahead performance, etc. To illustrate roll-forward partitioning, consider naive forecasts for the ridership data using either fixed partitioning (as shown in Figure 3.1) or month-by-month roll-forward partitioning (as in Table 3.2).

Figure 3.6 shows naive forecasts for the validation period, using a fixed 36-month validation period vs. one-step-ahead forecasts using a monthly roll-forward validation period. The fixed data partitioning produces a constant forecast for all 36 validation months (horizontal line), whereas the roll-forward partitioning produces one-month-ahead forecasts that get refreshed every month. We could potentially also draw the roll-forward two-steps-ahead forecasts, three-steps-ahead forecasts, etc.

Table 3.3 shows performance measures of the fixed and roll-forward partitioning approaches.

[9] Roll-forward validation that advances one period at a time is analogous to the notion of leave-one-out cross-validation in cross sectional data (see robjhyndman.com/hyndsight/crossvalidation)

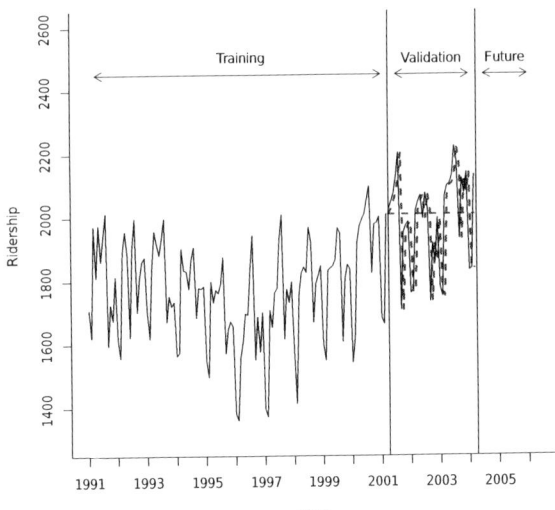

Figure 3.6: Naive forecasts using a fixed validation period (dashed horizontal line) vs. one-step-ahead naive forecasts using a monthly roll-forward validation period (other dashed line) for the Amtrak ridership data. The actual values in the validation period are plotted with a smooth line.

Method	MAE	RMSE	MAPE
Roll-forward one-month-ahead	119.429	169.173	6.206%
Roll-forward two-months-ahead	159.582	198.104	8.274%
⋮			
Roll-forward 36-month-ahead	124.518	124.518	5.839%
Roll-forward overall	157.760	190.416	7.972%
Fixed partitioning overall	115.923	142.755	6.021%

Table 3.3: Performance of naive forecasts using fixed partitioning vs. roll-forward partitioning, for one-month-ahead to 36-months-ahead forecasts

code for computing the predictive measures for roll-forward one-month-ahead forecasts in Table 3.3

```
fixed.nValid <- 36
fixed.nTrain <- length(ridership.ts) - fixed.nValid
stepsAhead <- 1
error <- rep(0, fixed.nValid - stepsAhead + 1)
percent.error <- rep(0, fixed.nValid - stepsAhead + 1)
for(j in fixed.nTrain:(fixed.nTrain + fixed.nValid - stepsAhead)) {
  train.ts <- window(ridership.ts, start = c(1991, 1), end = c(1991, j))
  valid.ts <- window(ridership.ts, start = c(1991, j + stepsAhead), end = c(1991, j + stepsAhead))
  naive.pred <- naive(train.ts, h = stepsAhead)
  error[j - fixed.nTrain + 1] <- valid.ts - naive.pred$mean[stepsAhead]
  percent.error[j - fixed.nTrain + 1] <- error[j - fixed.nTrain + 1] / valid.ts
}
mean(abs(error))
sqrt(mean(error^2))
mean(abs(percent.error))
```

Use a for loop and the window function to step through the differently sized training and validation sets. Use each training set to make a one-month-ahead naive forecast in the validation set by setting stepsAhead to one. Define two vectors of zeros to store the forecast errors and percentage errors. The last three lines calculate the predictive measures.

3.6 Example: Comparing Two Models

We introduce the following example in order to illustrate the notions of data partitioning, naive forecasts, and performance metrics, as well as how they are used in combination to compare models. Using the same Amtrak ridership data, we compare two methods: naive forecasts and seasonal naive forecasts.

Fixed Partitioning

We start with fixed partitioning, where the validation period is set to Apr 2001 - Mar 2004. The naive and seasonal naive forecasts for this validation period are shown in Table 3.4. We can then compute forecast errors and predictive measures based on these forecasts. A comparison of their predictive measures is shown in Table 3.5.

Period	Actual	Naive Forecast	Seasonal Naive Forecast
Apr 2001	2023.792	2007.928	1971.493
May 2001	2047.008	2007.928	1992.301
Jun 2001	2072.913	2007.928	2009.763
⋮	⋮	⋮	⋮
Mar 2004	2132.446	2007.928	2007.928

Table 3.4: Naive and seasonal naive forecasts for fixed validation period (ridership data)

Method	MAE	RMSE	MAPE
Naive Forecast	115.923	142.755	6.206%
Seasonal Naive Forecast	84.094	95.62433	4.248%

Table 3.5: Performance of naive vs. seasonal naive forecasts using fixed partitioning

code for computing naive and seasonal naive forecasts and their predictive measures

```
fixed.nValid <- 36
fixed.nTrain <- length(ridership.ts) - fixed.nValid
train.ts <- window(ridership.ts, start = c(1991, 1), end = c(1991, fixed.nTrain))
valid.ts <- window(ridership.ts, start = c(1991, fixed.nTrain + 1),
    end = c(1991, fixed.nTrain + fixed.nValid))
naive.pred <- naive(train.ts, h = fixed.nValid)
snaive.pred <- snaive(train.ts, h = fixed.nValid)
accuracy(naive.pred, valid.ts)
accuracy(snaive.pred, valid.ts)
```

Use the naive and snaive functions in the forecast package to create the naive and seasonal naive forecasts in the fixed validation period (as shown in Table 3.4). Use the accuracy function to find the predictive measures in Table 3.6.

Roll-Forward Partitioning

We now repeat the comparison of the two models (naive and seasonal naive), this time using the advanced partitioning method of roll-forward validation. We use the 36 data partitions shown in Table 3.2. For each partition, we use the naive and seasonal naive on the training period and generate one-step-ahead forecasts for the corresponding validation period. We have already seen the performance measures for the naive method in the first row of Table 3.3. Table 3.6 compares these measures to the seasonal naive forecast measures. We see that the seasonal naive forecasts outperform the naive forecasts on one-step-ahead forecasting. To compare the k-steps-ahead performance of these two models, we can adapt the R code that accompanies Table 3.3 by changing `stepsAhead` to the required value k.

Method	MAE	RMSE	MAPE
Naive Forecast	119.429	169.173	6.206%
Seasonal Naive Forecast	78.473	98.205	3.906%

Table 3.6: Performance of naive vs. seasonal naive one-step-ahead forecasts using roll-forward partitioning

3.7   Problems

1. *Souvenir Sales:* The file *SouvenirSales.xls* contains monthly sales for a souvenir shop at a beach resort town in Queensland, Australia, between 1995 and 2001. [source: Hyndman, R. J. Time Series Data Library, http://data.is/TSDLdemo; accessed on July 13, 2015.]

    Back in 2001, the store wanted to use the data to forecast sales for the next 12 months (year 2002). They hired an analyst to generate forecasts. The analyst first partitioned the data into training and validation periods, with the validation period containing the last 12 months of data (year 2001). She then fit a forecasting model to sales, using the training period.

    Partition the data into the training and validation periods as explained above.

    (a) Why were the data partitioned?

    (b) Why did the analyst choose a 12-month validation period?

    (c) What is the naive forecast for the validation period? (assume that you must provide forecasts for 12 months ahead)

    (d) Compute the RMSE and MAPE for the naive forecasts.

    (e) Plot a histogram of the forecast errors that result from the naive forecasts (for the validation period). Plot also a time

Figure 3.7: Image source: quyenlan / FreeDigitalPhotos.net

plot for the naive forecasts and the actual sales numbers in the validation period. What can you say about the behavior of the naive forecasts?

(f) The analyst found a forecasting model that gives satisfactory performance on the validation set. What must she do to use the forecasting model for generating forecasts for year 2002?

2. *Forecasting Shampoo Sales:* The file *ShampooSales.xls* contains data on the monthly sales of a certain shampoo over a three-year period. [source: Hyndman, R. J. Time Series Data Library, http://data.is/TSDLdemo; accessed on July 13, 2015.]

If the goal is forecasting sales in future months, which of the following steps should be taken? (choose one or more)

- partition the data into training and validation periods
- examine time plots of the series and of model forecasts only for the training period
- look at MAPE and RMSE values for the training period
- look at MAPE and RMSE values for the validation period
- compute naive forecasts

3. *Performance on Training and Validation Data:* Two different models were fit to the same time series. The first 100 time periods were used for the training period and the last 12 periods were treated as a validation period. Assume that both models make sense practically and fit the data reasonably well. Below are the RMSE values for each of the models:

	Training Period	Validation Period
Model A	543	690
Model B	669	675

(a) Which model appears more useful for retrospectively describing the different components of this time series? Why?

(b) Which model appears to be more useful for forecasting purposes? Why?

4
Forecasting Methods: Overview

Why is there such a variety of forecasting methods for time series? The answer is that different methods perform differently depending on the nature of the data and the forecasting requirements. Recall that an important benchmark to consider is naive forecasts (see Section 3.2). This simple approach is often powerful and should always be considered as a baseline for performance comparison of more sophisticated forecasting methods.

Before going into the details of particular forecasting methods, let us examine some of the differences underlying the major forecasting methods.

4.1 Model-Based vs. Data-Driven Methods

Forecasting methods can be roughly divided into model-based methods and data-driven methods.

Model-based methods use a statistical, mathematical, or other scientific model to approximate a data series. The training data are used to estimate the parameters of the model, and then the model with estimated parameters is used to generate forecasts. In Chapter 6 we describe model-based forecasting models such as multiple linear regression and autoregressive models, where the user specifies a certain linear model and then estimates it from the time series. Logistic regression models, as described in Chapter 7, are also model-based. Model-based methods are especially advantageous when the series at hand is very short. With an assumed underlying model, few data points are needed for estimating the model parameters.

Chapter 5 covers the data-driven approach of smoothing, where algorithms "learn" patterns from the data. Data-driven methods are advantageous when model assumptions are likely to be violated, or when the structure of the time series changes over time. Naive forecasts are also data-driven, in that they simply use the last data point in the series for generating a forecast. Another advantage of many data-driven forecasting methods is that they require less user input (and hence more "user proof") and are more easily automated. The lower user input, however, means that more data (that is, a longer series) is required for adequate learning. We also note that data mining methods such as neural networks (see Chapter 7), regression trees and other algorithms for predicting cross-sectional data are sometimes used for time series forecasting, especially for incorporating external information into the forecasts.[1]

Another difference between model-based and data-driven approaches relates to global vs. local patterns in the series. Model-based methods are generally preferable for forecasting series with global patterns that extend throughout the data period, as they use all the data to estimate the global pattern. For a local pattern, a model would require specifying how and when the patterns change, which is usually impractical and often unknown. Therefore, data-driven methods are preferable for forecasting series with local patterns. Such methods "learn" patterns from the data, and their memory length can be set to best adapt to the rate of change in the series. Patterns that change quickly warrant a "short memory", whereas patterns that change slowly warrant a "long memory".

4.2   Extrapolation Methods, Econometric Models, and External Information

The methods presented in this book create forecasts for a time series based on its history. Such methods are termed *extrapolation methods*. Naive forecasts are an example of extrapolation. In some applications, multiple related time series are to be forecasted simultaneously (e.g., the monthly sales of mul-

[1] For an example of using regression trees and random forests for time series forecasting, see the presentation by the winners of the "RTA Freeway Travel Time Prediction Challenge" at blog.kaggle.com/wp-content/uploads/2011/03/team_irazu_screencast.pdf.

tiple products), and it is expected that the values of one series are correlated with those of other series. Even in such cases, the most popular forecasting practice is to forecast each series using only its own historical values. The advantage of this practice is simplicity. The disadvantage is that forecasts do not take into account possible relationships between the series.

Econometric models approach cross-correlation between series from a causal standpoint, and often include information from one or more series as inputs into another series. Such models are based on assumptions of causality that are derived from theoretical models. An alternative approach is to capture the *associations* between the series of interest and model them directly into the forecasting method. The statistics literature contains models for *multivariate time series* that directly model the cross-correlations between a set of series. Such methods tend to make restrictive assumptions about the data and the cross-series structure, and they also require statistical expertise for estimation and maintenance.

A third alternative to both causal econometric models and multivariate time series models, when the purpose is forecasting, is to capture external information that correlates with a series more heuristically. An example is using the sales of lipstick to forecast some measure of the economy, based on the observation by Leonard Lauder, past chairman of Estee Lauder Companies Inc., that lipstick sales tend to increase before tough economic times (a phenomenon called the "leading lipstick indicator"). The most important factor to keep in mind is that whatever external information we integrate into the forecasting method, that information must be available at the time of prediction. For example, consider a model for forecasting the average weekly airfare on a certain route. The model uses weekly gas prices and past weekly airfare rates as inputs. Should we include only gas prices from past weeks or also from the week to be forecasted? The airfare forecast will obviously be more accurate if it is based on gas prices during the same week. However, that information is unavailable at the time of prediction! We could try and forecast gas prices, and include the forecast in the airfare model. However, it is obviously very difficult (and maybe impossible) to accurately forecast gas prices. In fact, if you are able to forecast gas prices accurately, you might no longer be interested in forecasting airfare... The moral is: *forecasting methods must only use values (or estimates) that are available at the time of prediction.*

In chapters 6 and 5 we focus on extrapolation methods. While smoothing methods are strictly extrapolation methods, regression models can be adapted to capture external information. Chapter 7 discusses the inclusion of external information into regression models and also introduces additional methods (logistic regression and neural networks) that can include external information.

4.3   Manual vs. Automated Forecasting

The level of required automation was briefly discussed in Chapter 1. In particular, the level of automation depends on the nature of the forecasting task and on how forecasts will be used in practice. More automation is usually required when many series are to be forecasted on a continuous basis, and not much forecasting expertise can be allocated to the process (recall the example of forecasting Point of Sale (POS) data for purposes of inventory control across many stores).

In terms of forecasting methods, some methods are easier to automate than others. Typically, data-driven methods are easier to automate, because they "learn" patterns from the data. Note, however, that even data driven methods can perform poorly if the characteristics of the series (seasonality, trend) are not correctly specified, or if there is insufficient data.

Model-based methods also range in their fitness for automation. Models that are based on many assumptions for producing adequate forecasts are less likely to be useful for automation, as they require constantly evaluating whether the assumptions are met. Similarly, models that fit global patterns can be automated only if they are evaluated periodically to check whether the patterns changed.

Data-driven methods such as smoothing methods (Chapter 5) are preferable for automated forecasting, because they require less tweaking, are suitable for a range of trends and seasonal patterns, are computationally fast, require very little data storage, and adjust when the behavior of a series changes over time. Neural networks (Chapter 7) are similarly useful for automation, although they are computationally more demanding and require all past data. One serious danger with data-driven methods is overfitting the training period, and hence performance should be carefully evaluated and constantly monitored to avoid this pitfall.

Even with an automated system in place, it is advisable to monitor the forecasts and forecast errors produced by an automated system and occasionally re-examine their suitability and update the system accordingly.

Finally, combined forecasts are usually good candidates for automated forecasting, because they are more robust to sensitivities of a single forecasting method. We discuss combined forecasts in the next section.

4.4   Combining Methods

While it might appear that one should choose one method for forecasting among the various options, it turns out that *combining multiple forecasting methods* can lead to improved predictive performance. Combining methods can be done via two-level (or multilevel) methods, where the first method uses the original time series to generate forecasts of future values, and the second method uses the forecast errors from the first layer to generate forecasts of future forecast errors, thereby "correcting" the first level forecasts. We describe two-level forecasting in Section 6.4.

Another combination approach is via *ensembles*, where multiple methods are applied to the time series, each generating separate forecasts. The resulting forecasts are then averaged in some way to produce the final forecast. Combining methods can take advantage of the capability of different forecasting methods to capture different aspects of the time series. For the same reason, ensembles are useful for predicting in cross-sectional settings. Averaging across multiple methods can lead to forecasts that are more robust and are of higher precision. Chapter 9 describes an ensemble approach used by the winner of a tourism forecasting competition.

Ensembles of predictions from multiple methods are also commonly used for predicting cross-sectional data. Ensembles played a major role in the million-dollar Netflix Prize[2] contest, where teams competed on creating the most accurate predictions of movie preferences by users of the Netflix DVD rental service. Different teams ended up joining forces to create ensemble predictions, which proved more accurate than the individual predictions. The winning team, called "BellKor's Pragmatic Chaos" combined results from the "BellKor" and "Big Chaos" teams alongside additional members. In a 2010 article in *Chance* magazine, the Netflix Prize winners described the power of their ensemble approach:

> An early lesson of the competition was the value of combining sets of predictions from multiple models or algorithms. If two prediction sets achieved similar RMSEs, it was quicker and more effective to simply average the two sets than to try to develop a new model that incorporated the best of each method. Even if the RMSE for one set was much worse than the other, there was almost certainly a linear combination that improved on the better set.[3]

[2] netflixprize.com

[3] R. M. Bell, Y. Koren, and C. Volinsky. All together now: A perspective on the Netflix Prize. *Chance*, 23:24–29, 2010

Figure 4.1: The 2009 Netflix Prize ensemble of winners. (Image courtesy of AT&T)

The principle of improving forecast precision (that is, reducing the variance of forecast errors) via ensembles is the same principle underlying the advantage of portfolios and diversification in financial investment. Improvement is greatest when the forecast errors are negatively correlated, or at least uncorrelated.

Finally, another combination approach is to use different series measuring the phenomenon of interest (e.g., temperature) and take an average of the multiple resulting forecasts. For example, when a series of interest is available from multiple sources, each with slightly different numbers or precision (e.g., from manual and electronic collection systems or from different departments or measuring devices), we can create ensembles of forecasts, each based on a different series. In the Amtrak ridership example, we might have daily passenger data collected manually from ticket collectors. Monthly ridership forecasts based on these data can be combined with forecasts from the monthly series collected by the electronic system. Of course, the performance of such an ensemble should be evaluated by comparing the ensemble forecasts against the actual values from the goal-defined series. In the Amtrak example, if forecast accuracy will eventually be measured against the official monthly ridership numbers reported to the Bureau of Transportation Statistics, then the ensemble forecasts should be evaluated relative to the same official ridership series (rather than relative to the manual ticket collector data).

The website www.forecastingprinciples.com, run and supported by forecasting experts, has a detailed Q&A page on combining forecasts.[4] The authors explain how and why ensembles improve forecast accuracy. To the question: "What are the disadvantages of combined forecasts?" they respond -

a) Increased costs

b) Need analysts who are familiar with a number of methods

c) Need to ensure that a pre-determined rule for combining is agreed upon. Otherwise, people can find a forecast to suit their biases.

They also address the question "Why isn't it common to use combined forecasts?" as follows:

a) It is counter-intuitive. People think you only get an average forecast and they believe that if they can pick a method, they

[4] forecastingprinciples.com/index.php?option=com_content&task=view&id=364&Itemid=6

will do better. (This explanation has been supported by experiments).

b) This solution is too simple. People like complex approaches.

4.5   Problems

1. A large medical clinic would like to forecast daily patient visits for purposes of staffing.

   (a) If data are available only for the last month, how does this affect the choice of model-based vs. data-driven methods?

   (b) The clinic has access to the admissions data of a nearby hospital. Under what conditions will including the hospital information be potentially useful for forecasting the clinic's daily visits?

   (c) Thus far, the clinic administrator takes a heuristic approach, using the visit numbers from the same day of the previous week as a forecast. What is the advantage of this approach? What is the disadvantage?

   (d) What level of automation appears to be required for this task? Explain.

   (e) Describe two approaches for improving the current heuristic (naive) forecasting approach using ensembles.

2. The ability to scale up renewable energy, and in particular wind power and speed, is dependent on the ability to forecast its short-term availability. Soman et al. (2010) describe different methods for wind power forecasting (the quote is slightly edited for brevity):[5]

   Persistence Method: This method is also known as 'Naive Predictor'. It is assumed that the wind speed at time $t + \delta t$ will be the same as it was at time t. Unbelievably, it is more accurate than most of the physical and statistical methods for very-short to short term forecasts...

   Physical Approach: Physical systems use parameterizations based on a detailed physical description of the atmosphere...

   Statistical Approach: The statistical approach is based on training with measurement data and uses difference between the predicted and the actual wind speeds in immediate past to tune model parameters. It is easy to model, inexpensive, and provides timely predictions. It is not based on any predefined mathematical model and rather it is based on patterns...

Figure 4.2: Image: Tina Phillips / FreeDigitalPhotos.net

[5] S. S. Soman, H. Zareipour, O. Malik, and P. Mandal. A review of wind power and wind speed forecasting methods with different time horizons. In *Proceedings of the 42nd North American Power Symposium (NAPS), Arlington, Texas, USA*, 2010

Hybrid Approach: In general, the combination of different approaches such as mixing physical and statistical approaches or combining short term and medium-term models, etc., is referred to as a hybrid approach.

(a) For each of the four types of methods, describe whether it is model-based, data-driven, or a combination.

(b) For each of the four types of methods, describe whether it is based on extrapolation, causal modeling, correlation modeling or a combination.

(c) Describe the advantages and disadvantages of the hybrid approach.

5
Smoothing Methods

In this chapter we describe popular, flexible methods for forecasting time series that rely on smoothing. Smoothing is based
on averaging over multiple observations in order to reduce the
noise. We start with two simple smoothers, the moving average
and simple exponential smoother, which are suitable for forecasting series that contain no trend or seasonality. In both cases
forecasts are averages of previous values of the series (the length
of the series history that is considered and the weights that are
used in the averaging differ between the methods). We also show
how a moving average can be used, with a slight adaptation, for
data visualization. We then proceed to describe smoothing methods that are suitable for forecasting series with a trend and/or
seasonality. Smoothing methods are data driven and are able
to adapt to changes in the series over time. Although highly
automated, the user must specify smoothing constants, which
determine how fast the method adapts to new data. We discuss
the choice of such constants and their meaning. The different
methods are illustrated using the Amtrak ridership series.

5.1   Introduction

Smoothing methods are a family of forecasting methods that
are data driven in the sense that they estimate time series components directly from the data without a predetermined structure. Data-driven methods are especially useful in series where
components change over time. Here we consider a type of data-

driven methods called "smoothing methods" or "smoothers". Such methods "smooth" out the noise in a series in an attempt to uncover the patterns. Smoothing is done by averaging over multiple observations, where different smoothers differ by the number of observations averaged, how the average is computed, how many times averaging is performed, and the like.

We now describe two types of smoothing methods that are popular in business applications due to their simplicity and adaptability: the moving average and exponential smoothing methods.

5.2   Moving Average

The moving average is a simple smoother; it consists of averaging across a window of consecutive observations, thereby generating a series of averages. A moving average with window width w means averaging across each set of w consecutive values, where w is determined by the user. In general, there are two types of moving averages: a centered moving average and a trailing moving average. Centered moving averages are powerful for visualizing trends because the averaging operation can suppress seasonality and noise, thereby making the trend more visible. In contrast, trailing moving averages are useful for forecasting. The difference between the two is the placement of the averaging window over the time series.

Centered Moving Average for Visualization

In a centered moving average, the value of the moving average at time t (MA_t) is computed by centering the window around time t and averaging across the w values within the window:

$$MA_t = \left(y_{t-(w-1)/2} + \cdots + y_{t-1} + y_t + y_{t+1} + \cdots + y_{t+(w-1)/2} \right) / w. \tag{5.1}$$

For example, with a window of width $w = 5$, the moving average at time point $t = 3$ means averaging the values of the series at time points 1, 2, 3, 4, 5; at time point $t = 4$ the moving average is the average of the series at time points 2, 3, 4, 5, 6, and so on. This is illustrated in the top panel of Figure 5.1.

Figure 5.1: Schematic of centered moving average (top) and trailing moving average (bottom), both with window width $w = 5$

Choosing the window width in a seasonal series is straight-forward: because the goal is to suppress seasonality for better visualizing the trend, the default choice should be the length of a seasonal cycle. Returning to the Amtrak ridership data, the annual seasonality indicates a choice of $w = 12$. Figure 5.2 shows a centered moving average line overlaid on the original series. We can see a global U-shape, but the moving average shows some deviation from this shape, such as the slight dip during the last year.

Trailing Moving Average for Forecasting

Centered moving averages are computed by averaging across data both in the past and future of a given time point. In that sense, they cannot be used for forecasting because at the time of forecasting, the future is typically unknown. Hence, for purposes of forecasting, we use trailing moving averages, where the window of width w is set on the most recent available w values of the series. The k-step-ahead forecast F_{t+k} ($k = 1, 2, 3, \ldots$) is then the average of these w values (see also bottom plot in Figure 5.1):

$$F_{t+k} = \left(y_t + y_{t-1} + \cdots + y_{t-w+1} \right) / w. \qquad (5.2)$$

For example, in the Amtrak ridership series, to forecast ridership in February 1992 or later months, given information until January 1992 and using a moving average with window width $w=12$, we would take the average ridership during the most recent 12 months (February 1991 to January 1992).

Next we illustrate a 12-month moving average forecaster for the Amtrak ridership. We partition once again the Amtrak ridership time series, leaving the last 36 months as the validation

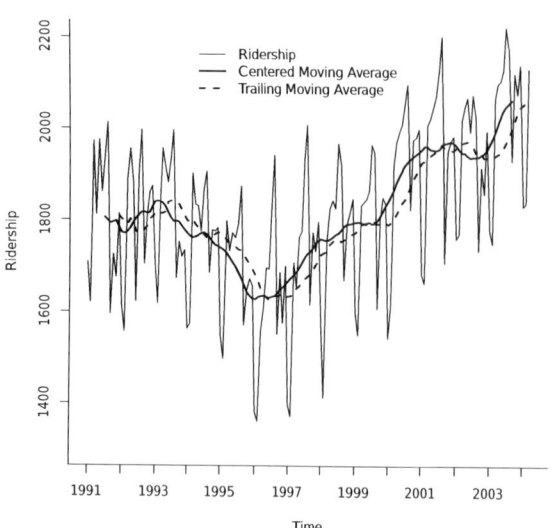

Figure 5.2: Centered moving average (smooth black line) and trailing moving average (broken black line) with window $w = 12$, overlaid on Amtrak ridership series

 code for creating Figure 5.2

```
library("zoo")
ma.trailing <- rollmean(ridership.ts, k = 12, align = "right")
ma.centered <- ma(ridership.ts, order = 12)
plot(ridership.ts, ylim = c(1300, 2200),  ylab = "Ridership", xlab = "Time", bty = "l", xaxt = "n",
    xlim = c(1991,2004.25), main = "")
axis(1, at = seq(1991, 2004.25, 1), labels = format(seq(1991, 2004.25, 1)))
lines(ma.centered, lwd = 2)
lines(ma.trailing, lwd = 2, lty = 2)
legend(1994,2200, c("Ridership","Centered Moving Average", "Trailing Moving Average"), lty=c(1,1,2),
    lwd=c(1,2,2), bty = "n")
```

Install and load the zoo package. Its rollmean function will calculate a trailing moving average according to Equation 5.2 when the argument align is set to "right". The function ma in the forecast package creates a centered moving average. The arguments k and order are the respective windows of these moving averages. In the function ma when order is an even number, the centered moving average is the average of two asymmetric moving averages. For instance, when order = 4, $MA_t = [(y_{t-2} + y_{t-1} + y_t + y_{t+1})/4 + (y_{t-1} + y_t + y_{t+1} + y_{t+2})/4]/2$. When order is odd, the centered moving average is comprised of one symmetric moving average according to Equation 5.1.

period. Applying a moving average forecaster with window $w = 12$, we obtained the output partially shown in Figure 5.3. Note that for the first 12 records of the training period, there is no forecast (because there are less than 12 past values to average). Also, note that the forecasts for all months in the validation period are identical (1938.481) because the method assumes that information is known only until March 2001. In other words, the validation forecasts are *not* roll-forward next-month forecasts.

In this example, it is clear that the moving average forecaster is inadequate for generating monthly forecasts because it does not capture the seasonality in the data. Seasons with high ridership are under-forecasted, and seasons with low ridership are over-forecasted. A similar issue arises when forecasting a series with a trend: the moving average "lags behind", thereby under-forecasting in the presence of an increasing trend and over-forecasting in the presence of a decreasing trend. This "lagging behind" of the trailing moving average can also be seen in Figure 5.2.

In general, the moving average can be used for forecasting only in series that lack seasonality and trend. Such a limitation might seem impractical. However, there are a few popular methods for removing trends (*de-trending*) and removing seasonality (*deseasonalizing*) from a series, such as regression models (Chapter 6), advanced exponential smoothing methods (Section 5.5), and the operation of *differencing* (Section 5.3). The moving average can then be used to forecast such de-trended and de-seasonalized series, and then the trend and seasonality can be added back to the forecast.

Choosing Window Width (w)

With moving average forecasting or visualization, the only choice that the user must make is the width of the window (w). As with other data-driven methods, the choice of the smoothing parameter is a balance between under-smoothing and over-smoothing. For visualization (using a centered window), wider windows will expose more global trends, while narrow windows will reveal local trend. Hence, examining several window widths

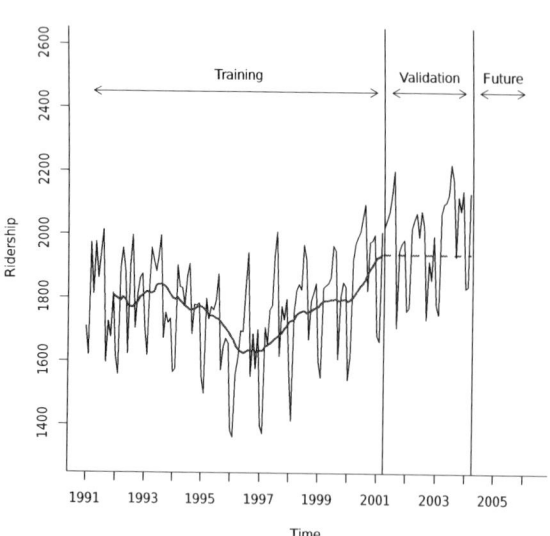

Figure 5.3: Trailing moving average forecaster with $w = 12$ applied to Amtrak ridership series.

 code for creating Figure 5.3

```
nValid <- 36
nTrain <- length(ridership.ts) - nValid
train.ts <- window(ridership.ts, start = c(1991, 1), end = c(1991, nTrain))
valid.ts <- window(ridership.ts, start = c(1991, nTrain + 1), end = c(1991, nTrain + nValid))
ma.trailing <- rollmean(train.ts, k = 12, align = "right")
last.ma <- tail(ma.trailing, 1)
ma.trailing.pred <- ts(rep(last.ma, nValid), start = c(1991, nTrain + 1),
    end = c(1991, nTrain + nValid), freq = 12)
plot(train.ts, ylim = c(1300, 2600), ylab = "Ridership", xlab = "Time", bty = "l", xaxt = "n",
    xlim = c(1991,2006.25), main = "")
axis(1, at = seq(1991, 2006, 1), labels = format(seq(1991, 2006, 1)))
lines(ma.trailing, lwd = 2, col = "blue")
lines(ma.trailing.pred, lwd = 2, col = "blue", lty = 2)
lines(valid.ts)
```

Set up the training and validation sets using fixed partitioning. Use the rollmean function to create the trailing moving average over the training period. With the tail function, find the last moving average in the training period, and use it repeatedly as the prediction for each month in the validation period. Plot the time series in the training and validation periods, the moving average over the training period, and the predictions for the validation period.

is useful for exploring trends of differing local/global nature. For forecasting (using a trailing window), the choice should incorporate some domain knowledge in terms of relevance of past observations and how fast the series changes. Empirical predictive evaluation can also be done by experimenting with different values of w and comparing performance. However, care should be taken not to overfit!

Note: A trailing moving average with $w = 1$ generates naive forecasts, while $w = n$ (the length of the training period) means using the average of the series over the entire training period.

5.3   Differencing

A simple and popular method for removing a trend and/or a seasonal pattern from a series is by the operation of *differencing*. Differencing means taking the difference between two observations. A lag-1 difference (also called first difference) means taking the difference between every two consecutive values in the series $(y_t - y_{t-1})$.[1] Differencing at lag-k means subtracting the value from k periods back $(y_t - y_{t-k})$. For example, for a daily series, lag-7 differencing means subtracting from each value (y_t) the value on the same day in the previous week (y_{t-7}).

[1] In R, a lag-12 difference of the Amtrak ridership is created by running `diff(ridership.ts, lag = 12)`.

To remove trends and seasonal patterns we can difference the original time series and obtain a differenced series that lacks trend and seasonality. Lag-1 differencing results in a differenced series that measures the changes from one period to the next.

Removing Trend (De-trending)

lag-1 differencing is useful for removing a trend. An example of the Amtrak lag-1 differenced series is shown in the bottom left panel of Figure 5.4. Compared to the original series (top left panel), which exhibits a U-shaped trend, the lag-1 differenced series contains no visible trend. One advantage of differencing over other methods (e.g., a regression with a trend - see Chapter 6) is that differencing does not assume that the trend is global, i.e., that the trend is fixed throughout the entire period.

Ridership

Lag–12 Difference

Lag–1 Difference

Twice–Differenced (Lag–12, Lag–1)

Figure 5.4: Differencing the Amtrak ridership series. Top left: original series with trend and seasonality. Bottom left: lag-1 differenced series. Top right: lag-12 differenced series. Bottom right: twice differenced series (lag-12 then lag-1)

For quadratic and exponential trends, often another round of lag-1 differencing must be applied in order to remove the trend. This means taking lag-1 differences of the differenced series.

Removing Seasonality (Seasonal Adjustment, Deseasonalizing)

For removing a seasonal pattern with M seasons, we difference at lag M. For example, to remove a day-of-week pattern in daily data, we can take lag- 7 differences. Figure 5.4 (top right panel) illustrates a lag-12 differenced series of the Amtrak monthly data. The monthly pattern no longer appears in this differenced series.

Removing Trend and Seasonality

When both trend and seasonality exist, we can apply differencing twice to the series in order to de-trend and deseasonalize it. We performed double differencing on the Amtrak data, which contain both trend and seasonality. The bottom right panel of Figure 5.4 shows the result after first differencing at lag-12, and then applying a lag-1 difference to the differenced series.[2] The result is a series with no trend and no monthly seasonality.

Note: Differencing is often used as a pre-processing step before applying a forecasting model to a series. However, when the forecasting method is a data-driven artificial intelligence algorithm such as neural networks (see Chapter 7), differencing appears to produce inferior results compared to including lag variables as predictors.[3]

5.4 Simple Exponential Smoothing

A popular forecasting method in business is exponential smoothing. Its popularity derives from its flexibility, ease of automation, cheap computation, and good performance. Simple exponential smoothing is similar to forecasting with a moving average, except that instead of taking a simple average over the w most recent values, we take a *weighted average* of *all* past values, so that the weights decrease exponentially into the past. The idea is to

[2] In R, this twice differencing is created by running `diff(diff(ridership.ts, lag = 12), lag = 1)`.

[3] N. K. Ahmed, A. F. Atiya, N. El Gayar, and H. El-Shishiny. An empirical comparison of machine learning models for time series forecasting. *Econometric Reviews*, 29:594–621, 2010

give more weight to recent information, yet not to completely ignore older information. Like the moving average, simple exponential smoothing should only be used for *forecasting series that have no trend or seasonality*. As mentioned earlier, such series can be obtained by removing trend and/or seasonality from raw series, and then applying exponential smoothing to the series of residuals (which are assumed to contain no trend or seasonality).

The exponential smoother generates a forecast at time $t+1$ (F_{t+1}) as follows:

$$F_{t+1} = \alpha y_t + \alpha(1-\alpha)y_{t-1} + \alpha(1-\alpha)^2 y_{t-2} + \cdots \quad (5.3)$$

where α is a constant between 0 and 1 called the *smoothing constant*. The above formulation displays the exponential smoother as a weighted average of all past observations, with exponentially decaying weights.

We can also write the exponential forecaster in another way, which is very useful in practice:

$$F_{t+1} = F_t + \alpha e_t, \quad (5.4)$$

where e_t is the forecast error at time t. This formulation presents the exponential forecaster as an "active learner". It looks at the previous forecast (F_t) and at its distance from the actual value (e_t), and then corrects the next forecast based on that information. If the forecast was too high in the last period, the next period is adjusted down. The amount of correction depends on the value of the smoothing constant α. The formulation in Equation (5.4) is also advantageous in terms of data storage and computation time: we need to store and use only the forecast and forecast error from the previous period, rather than the entire series. In applications where real-time forecasting is done, or many series are being forecasted in parallel and continuously, such savings are critical.

Note that forecasting further into the future yields the same forecasts as a one-step-ahead forecast. Because the series is assumed to lack trend and seasonality, forecasts into the future rely only on information that is available at the time of prediction. Hence, the k-step-ahead forecast is given by $F_{t+k} = F_{t+1}$.

Choosing Smoothing Constant α

The smoothing constant α, which is set by the user, determines the rate of learning. A value close to 1 indicates fast learning (that is, only the most recent observations have influence on forecasts), whereas a value close to 0 indicates slow learning (past observations have a large influence on forecasts). This can be seen by plugging 0 or 1 into the two equations above (5.3-5.4). Hence, the choice of α depends on the required amount of smoothing, and on how relevant the history is for generating forecasts. Default values that have been shown to work well are in the range 0.1-0.2. Trial and error can also help in the choice of α. Examine the time plot of the actual and predicted series, as well as the predictive accuracy (e.g., MAPE or RMSE of the validation period).

Finding the α value that optimizes one-step-ahead predictive accuracy over the training period can be used to determine the degree of local versus global nature of the level. However, beware of choosing the "best α" for forecasting, as this can lead to model overfitting and low predictive accuracy over the validation period and/or future.

In R, forecasting using simple exponential smoothing can be done via the ets function in the forecast package. The three letters in ets stand for *error*, *trend*, and *seasonality*, respectively. Applying this function to a time series will yield forecasts and forecast errors (residuals) for both the training and validation periods. You can use a default value of α=0.2, set it to another value, or choose to find the optimal α in terms of minimizing RMSE over the training period.[4]

To illustrate forecasting with simple exponential smoothing, we use the twice-differenced Amtrak ridership data in the bottom right panel of Figure 5.4, which are assumed to contain no trend or seasonality. To make forecasts in the validation period, we fit the simple exponential smoothing model to the training set (February 1992 to March 2001) with α=0.2. The simple exponential smoothing model in the ets framework is the model with additive error (A), no trend (N), and no seasonality (N). In the ets function, we set model = "ANN" in order to fit this model.

[4] The ets function chooses the optimal α and initial level value by maximizing something called the *likelihood* over the training period. In the case of simple exponential smoothing model, maximizing the *likelihood* is equivalent to minimizing the RMSE in the training period (the RMSE in the training period is equal to σ, the standard deviation of the training residuals.)

The forecasts of this model are shown in Figure 5.5. The forecast of the twice-differenced series for each month in the validation period is -6.345104. These forecasts are below zero because more recently the level of the series has been negative.

Next we compare the performance of the simple exponential smoothing model with α=0.2 to the one with an optimally chosen α. Table 5.1 provides a summary of the optimal model, followed by a comparison of its performance to the model with α=0.2. In the case of the twice-differenced Amtrak ridership data, the optimally chosen α is essentially zero ($\alpha = 1e - 04$ is scientific notation for 0.0001, which is the lowest possible value the ets function considers). This choice means that the level is global. The global level (also the initial state l according to the ets function) is 1.6583. Because this level is global, it is the model's forecast for each month in the validation period. Compared to the model with α=0.2, the optimal model has a lower RMSE in both the training set and the validation set (called the "test set" by the accuracy function).

We leave it to the reader to investigate the other items provided in the reports from the ets and accuracy functions.[5]

[5] See the online textbook *Forecasting: Principles and Practice* by Hyndman and Athanasopoulos at www.otexts.org/fpp.

Relationship Between Moving Average and Simple Exponential Smoothing

In both smoothing methods the user must specify a single parameter: in moving averages, the window width (w) must be set and in exponential smoothing, the smoothing constant (α) must be set. In both cases, the parameter determines the importance of fresh information over older information. In fact, the two smoothers are approximately equal if the window width of the moving average is equal to $w = 2/\alpha - 1$.

5.5   Advanced Exponential Smoothing

As mentioned earlier, both moving average and simple exponential smoothing should only be used for forecasting series with no trend or seasonality; series that have only a level and noise. One solution for forecasting series with trend and/or seasonality is

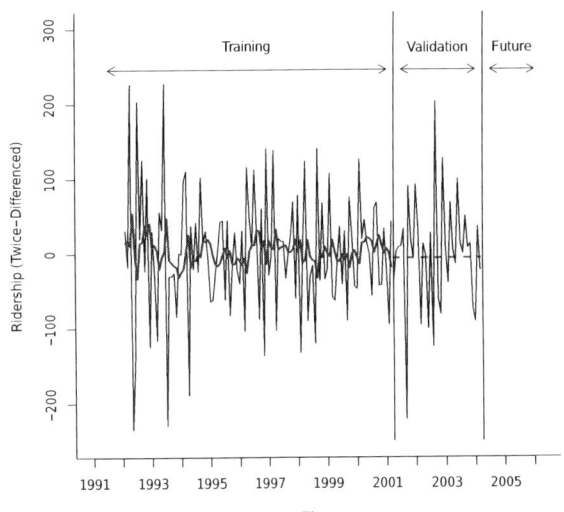

Figure 5.5: Forecasts
from a simple exponen-
tial smoothing forecaster
with α=0.2, applied to the
twice-differenced Amtrak
ridership data (which lack
trend and seasonality).

 code for creating Figure 5.5

```
diff.twice.ts <- diff(diff(ridership.ts, lag = 12), lag = 1)

nValid <- 36
nTrain <- length(diff.twice.ts) - nValid
train.ts <- window(diff.twice.ts, start = c(1992, 2), end = c(1992, nTrain + 1))
valid.ts <- window(diff.twice.ts, start = c(1992, nTrain + 2), end = c(1992, nTrain + 1 + nValid))

ses <- ets(train.ts, model = "ANN", alpha = 0.2)
ses.pred <- forecast(ses, h = nValid, level = 0)
ses.pred

plot(ses.pred, ylim = c(-250, 300),  ylab = "Ridership (Twice-Differenced)", xlab = "Time",
    bty = "l", xaxt = "n", xlim = c(1991,2006.25), main = "", flty = 2)
axis(1, at = seq(1991, 2006, 1), labels = format(seq(1991, 2006, 1)))
lines(ses.pred$fitted, lwd = 2, col = "blue")
lines(valid.ts)
```

Set up the training and validation sets using fixed partitioning. Use the ets function with
the options model = "ANN" and alpha = 0.2 to fit a simple exponential smoothing model
over the training period. Use the forecast function to make predictions using this ses
model for h = nValid steps-ahead in the validation period. Print these predictions in tabu-
lar form and then plot them.

```
> ses.opt
ETS(A,N,N)
Call: ets(y = train.ts, model = "ANN")
  Smoothing parameters:
    alpha = 1e-04
  Initial states:
   l = 1.6583
  sigma:  82.8209
     AIC     AICc      BIC
1492.723 1492.835 1498.124
```

Table 5.1: Comparison of performance of two simple exponential smoothing models, fit to the twice-differenced Amtrak ridership data. The optimal model, ses.opt, is summarized first.

```
> accuracy(ses.pred, valid.ts)
                    ME     RMSE      MAE      MPE     MAPE      MASE       ACF1 Theil's U
Training set -0.9407425 90.82254 68.01782 181.35457 225.2854 0.6669040 -0.3678952      NA
Test set      5.7226043 75.99033 54.88964  55.92139 178.3106 0.5381843 -0.3665235   1.113
> accuracy(ses.opt.pred, valid.ts)
                     ME     RMSE      MAE      MPE     MAPE      MASE       ACF1 Theil's U
Training set -0.001116552 82.82094 62.90416 100.5652 106.3611 0.6167654 -0.3398588      NA
Test set     -2.280828663 75.80886 53.02528 111.5202 111.5202 0.5199045 -0.3665235 0.9627726
```

 code for creating Table 5.1

```
ses.opt <- ets(train.ts, model = "ANN")
ses.opt.pred <- forecast(ses.opt, h = nValid, level = 0)
accuracy(ses.pred, valid.ts)
accuracy(ses.opt.pred, valid.ts)
ses.opt
```

Use the ets function with the option model = "ANN" to fit a simple exponential smoothing model where α is chosen optimally. Use the forecast function to make predictions using this ses.opt model for h = nValid steps-ahead in the validation period. Compare the two models' performance metrics using the accuracy function in the forecast package. The last line provides a summary of the ses.opt model.

first to remove those components (e.g., via differencing). Another solution is to use a more sophisticated version of exponential smoothing, which can capture trend and/or seasonality.

Series with an Additive Trend

For series that contain a trend, we can use *double exponential smoothing*, also called Holt's linear trend model. The trend in this model is not assumed to be global, but rather it can change over time.[6] In double exponential smoothing, the local trend is estimated from the data and is updated as more data become available. Similar to simple exponential smoothing, the level of the series is also estimated from the data, and is updated as more data become available. The k-step-ahead forecast is given by combining the level estimate at time t (L_t) and the trend estimate (which is assumed additive) at time t (T_t):

$$F_{t+k} = L_t + kT_t. \qquad (5.5)$$

Note that in the presence of a trend, one- two- three-step-ahead (etc.) forecasts are no longer identical. The level and trend are updated through a pair of updating equations:

$$
\begin{aligned}
L_t &= \alpha y_t + (1-\alpha)(L_{t-1} + T_{t-1}), & (5.6)\\
T_t &= \beta(L_t - L_{t-1}) + (1-\beta)T_{t-1}. & (5.7)
\end{aligned}
$$

The first equation means that the level at time t is a weighted average of the actual value at time t and the level in the previous period, adjusted for trend (in the presence of a trend, moving from one period to the next requires factoring in the trend). The second equation means that the trend at time t is a weighted average of the trend in the previous period and the more recent information on the change in level.[7] Two smoothing constants, α and β, determine the rate of learning. As in simple exponential smoothing, they are both constants between 0 and 1, set by the user, with higher values giving faster learning (more weight to most recent information).

Before moving on to discuss another type of trend, we introduce the two types of errors an exponential smoothing model

[6] This is in contrast to linear regression - see Chapter 6.

[7] There are various ways to estimate the initial values L_0 and T_0, but the difference between estimates usually disappears after a few periods. Note that R's ets function uses the notation l for level and b for trend.

can capture. The first type is an additive error. It means that y_{t+1} consists not only of level+trend but also an additional error:

$$y_{t+1} = L_t + T_t + e_t. \qquad (5.8)$$

In the additive error case, the errors are assumed to have a fixed magnitude, irrespective of the current level+trend of the series. If, however, it is more reasonable that the size of the error grows as the level of the series increases, then we will want to use a multiplicative error:

$$y_{t+1} = (L_t + T_t) \times (1 + e_t). \qquad (5.9)$$

Here the error acts as a percentage increase in the current level-plus-trend. In R, we can choose to include either an additive error or a multiplicative error in an additive trend model (without seasonality). To do so, we include either the option model = "AAN" or model = "MAN" in the ets function. Recall that the first letter in the model option refers to the error type.

Series with a Multiplicative Trend

The additive trend model assumes that the level changes from one period to the next by a fixed amount. Hence, the forecasting equation (5.5) adds k trend estimates. In contrast, a multiplicative trend model assumes that the level changes from one period to the next by a factor. Exponential smoothing with a multiplicative trend therefore produces k-step-ahead forecasts using the formula

$$F_{t+k} = L_t \times T_t^k. \qquad (5.10)$$

and the updating equations for the level and trend are

$$L_t = \alpha y_t + (1 - \alpha)(L_{t-1} \times T_{t-1}), \qquad (5.11)$$
$$T_t = \beta(L_t/L_{t-1}) + (1 - \beta)T_{t-1}. \qquad (5.12)$$

As with the additive trend model, we can include either an additive or multiplicative error in the multiplicative trend model. The additive error takes the form

$$y_{t+1} = L_t \times T_t + e_t, \qquad (5.13)$$

while the multiplicative error takes the form

$$y_{t+1} = (L_t \times T_t) \times (1 + e_t). \tag{5.14}$$

With the ets function in R, we can include either an additive error or a multiplicative error in the multiplicative trend model (without seasonality) using the option model = "AMN" or model = "MMN", respectively.

Series with a Trend and Seasonality

For series that contain both trend and seasonality, the *Holt-Winter's exponential smoothing* method can be used. This is a further extension of double exponential smoothing, where the k-step-ahead forecast also takes into account the season at period $t + k$. As for trend, there exist formulations for additive and multiplicative seasonality. In *multiplicative seasonality*, values on different seasons differ by percentage amounts, whereas in *additive seasonality*, they differ by a fixed amount.

Assuming seasonality with M seasons (e.g., for weekly seasonality $M = 7$), the forecast for an additive trend and multiplicative seasonality is given by:

$$F_{t+k} = (L_t + kT_t)S_{t+k-M}. \tag{5.15}$$

(Note that by the forecasting time t, the series must have included at least a full cycle of seasons in order to produce forecasts using this formula, i.e., $t > M$).

Being an adaptive method, Holt-Winter's exponential smoothing allows the level, trend, and seasonality patterns to change over time. The three components are estimated and updated as new information arrives. The updating equations for this additive trend and multiplicative seasonality version are given by:

$$
\begin{align}
L_t &= \alpha y_t / S_{t-M} + (1 - \alpha)(L_{t-1} + T_{t-1}) \tag{5.16} \\
T_t &= \beta(L_t - L_{t-1}) + (1 - \beta)T_{t-1} \tag{5.17} \\
S_t &= \gamma (y_t / L_t) + (1 - \gamma)S_{t-M}. \tag{5.18}
\end{align}
$$

The first equation is similar to that in double exponential smoothing, except that it uses the seasonally adjusted value at time t

rather than the raw value. This is done by dividing y_t by its seasonal index, as estimated in the last cycle. The second equation is identical to double exponential smoothing. The third equation means that the seasonal index is updated by taking a weighted average of the seasonal index from the previous cycle and the current trend-adjusted value.

The *additive seasonality* version of Holt-Winter's exponential smoothing, where seasons differ by a constant amount, can be constructed from the multiplicative version by replacing multiplication/division signs by addition/subtraction signs for the seasonal component:

$$F_{t+k} = L_t + kT_t + S_{t+k-M} \tag{5.19}$$
$$L_t = \alpha (y_t - S_{t-M}) + (1 - \alpha)(L_{t-1} + T_{t-1}) \tag{5.20}$$
$$T_t = \beta(L_t - L_{t-1}) + (1 - \beta)T_{t-1} \tag{5.21}$$
$$S_t = \gamma (y_t - L_t) + (1 - \gamma)S_{t-M} \tag{5.22}$$

To illustrate forecasting a series with an additive trend and multiplicative seasonality using Holt-Winter's method, consider the raw Amtrak ridership data. As we observed earlier, the data contain both a trend and monthly seasonality. Figure 5.6 depicts the fitted and forecasted values from the ets function in R.

Table 5.2 presents a summary of the model in Figure 5.6. After the call, we see estimates of the three smoothing parameters and the initial states of the level (l), trend (b), and seasonal components (s) in reverse order from December to January. Because α is far from zero, we conclude that the level adapts locally, while the trend is global (β is near zero), and seasonality appears global (γ is very near zero). A print out of the final states (which we get by running hw$states[nrow(hw$states),]) indicates that the seasonality indices have changed very little from their initial estimates. The final seasonal indexes are in reverse order from the last month in the training set (i.e., from s1=March to s12=April). In addition to identifying a global seasonal pattern, we notice that the trough and peak seasons are February and August, respectively. February is 85.38% of the non-seasonal forecast, and August is 111.43% of non-seasonal forecast.

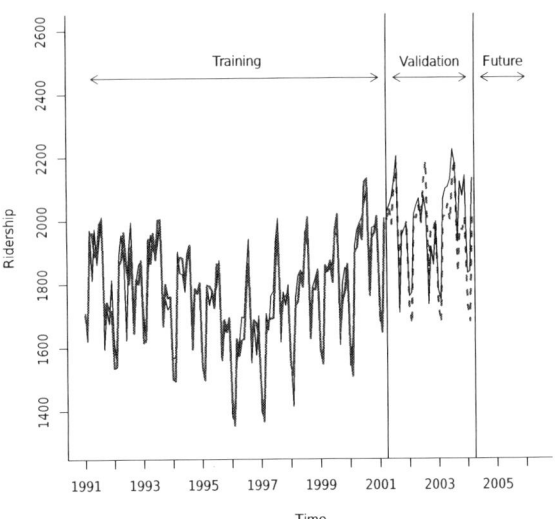

Figure 5.6: Forecasts from the Holt-Winter's exponential smoothing applied to the Amtrak ridership series. The training and validation sets, train.ts and valid.ts, come from the R code for creating Figure 5.3.

 code for creating Figure 5.6

```
hw <- ets(train.ts, model = "AAM", restrict = FALSE)
hw.pred <- forecast(hw, h = nValid, level = 0)

plot(hw.pred, ylim = c(1300, 2600),  ylab = "Ridership", xlab = "Time", bty = "l", xaxt = "n",
    xlim = c(1991,2006.25), main = "", flty = 2)
axis(1, at = seq(1991, 2006, 1), labels = format(seq(1991, 2006, 1)))
lines(hw.pred$fitted, lwd = 2, col = "blue")
lines(valid.ts)
```

Use the ets function with the options model = "AAM" and restrict = FALSE to fit Holt-Winter's exponential smoothing model with additive error, additive trend, and multiplicative seasonality. Use the forecast function to make predictions using this hw model for h = nValid steps-ahead in the validation period. Plot these predictions and print out a summary of the model.

```
> hw
ETS(A,A,M)
Call: ets(y = train.ts, model = "AAM", restrict = FALSE)
  Smoothing parameters:
    alpha = 0.6952
    beta  = 0.0069
    gamma = 3e-04
  Initial states:
    l = 1937.0504
    b = -3.01
    s=1.0199 1.0008 1.0049 0.9316 1.1143 1.0842
          1.0164 1.0438 1.0248 1.0252 0.8538 0.8803
  sigma:   56.9133
      AIC      AICc      BIC
1618.115 1623.247 1663.110
> hw$states[nrow(hw$states), ]
            l            b           s1           s2           s3           s4           s5
1953.7144508    0.3935235    1.0251793    0.8537774    0.8803079    1.0198736    1.0007752
           s6           s7           s8           s9          s10          s11          s12
   1.0048729    0.9316540    1.1143275    1.0842233    1.0164194    1.0438320    1.0248376
```

Table 5.2: Comparison of performance of two simple exponential smoothing models, fit to the twice-differenced Amtrak ridership data. The optimal model, ses.opt, is summarized first.

5.6   Summary of Exponential Smoothing in R Using ets

For the additive seasonality and multiplicative seasonality versions of the exponential smoothing model introduced above, we can include either an additive or multiplicative error. We can also specify an additive trend, a multiplicative trend, or no trend at all. This flexibility of the ets function in R gives us 18 models from which to choose: 2 error types × 3 trend types × 3 seasonality types.

There are two other trend types that the ets function allows: the additive damped trend (Ad) and the multiplicative damped trend (Md). These advanced trend types apply to time series whose trends will eventually dampen to a flat line in the distant future.[8] By including these two other trend types, the number of possible models the ets function can fit increases to 30. These models are summarized in Table 5.3 where the error (Z) can be either set to additive (A) or multiplicative (M).

We note that the ets function by default restricts the use of some models in Table 5.3. It does so because some combinations of error, trend, and seasonality can cause numerical difficulties when fit to some time series. For instance, ets function will not

[8] For more information on these advanced trend types, see Section 7/4 of the online textbook *Forecasting: Principles and Practice* by Hyndman and Athanasopoulos at www.otexts.org/fpp/7/4.

Trend	Seasonality		
	None	Additive	Multiplicative
None	ZNN	ZNA	ZNM
Additive	ZAN	ZAA	ZAM
Multiplicative	ZMN	ZMA	ZMM
Additive damped	ZAdN	ZAdA	ZAdM
Multiplicative damped	ZMdN	ZMdA	ZMdM

Table 5.3: Possible exponential smoothing models in R where Z can be set to A or M, corresponding to additive or multiplicative seasonality, respectively.

fit the AAM model unless we turn the restriction off by including the option restrict = FALSE in the ets function. In our illustration of the AAM model above (Figure 5.6), the estimation of the model seemed to work just fine. When you fit a restricted model, check that the results seem plausible.

Automated Model Selection in ets

If you do not know which model to choose, you can use the ets function to do automated model selection. By leaving out the model option altogether or by using model = "ZZZ", the function will fit several models (but not the restricted ones) and choose the "best" one. You can also automatically select a model from a subset of models by putting a Z in one or two places in the model specification. For instance, you can automated select the best additive error model by setting model = "AZZ".

How does ets define "best" for choosing between models with different numbers of parameters? It uses a criterion called Akaike's Information Criterion (AIC), which combines fit to the training data with a penalty for the number of smoothing parameters and initial values (L_0, T_0, etc.) included in a model.[9] The AIC criterion penalizes a model for having low fit to the training period and for being more complicated. Recall that simpler models (those with few smoothing parameters/initial states) can help avoid overfitting a model to the training set and hence can improve predictions in the validation period or the future.

The output from applying automated model selection to the Amtrak ridership data is shown in Table 5.4. The MNA model se-

[9] AIC is defined as:

$$AIC = -log(likelihood) + 2p$$

where *likelihood* is a measure of fit to the training period and p is the number of smoothing parameters and initial states in the model. The concept is similar to adjusted-R^2 used in regression models, which combines the model's fit with a penalty on the number of parameters.

lected has multiplicative error, no trend, and additive seasonality. Its AIC is 1608.976, which is 9.139 lower than the AAM model fit using the R code for creating Figure 5.6. As a rule of thumb, an AIC difference between 0 and 2 does not favor (not even weakly) one model or the other. Here, an AIC difference of 9.139 strongly favors the MNA model.

```
> ets(train.ts)
ETS(M,N,A)
Call: ets(y = train.ts)
  Smoothing parameters:
    alpha = 0.5653
    gamma = 1e-04
  Initial states:
    l = 1899.2864
    s=25.8874 -10.448 -0.6701 -122.7463 199.0173 150.1639
          42.8476 82.9771 52.7806 48.1995 -254.7762 -213.2329
  sigma:   0.0316
      AIC      AICc      BIC
 1608.976 1612.865 1648.347
```

Table 5.4: Automated model selection applied to the Amtrak ridership data. The training set train.ts comes from the R code for creating Figure 5.3.

Finally, a word of caution about automated model selection is in order. Although it can be tempting to automate the hard work of model selection, our practical experience suggests that it is better to compare the performance of several models on the validation set (using either fixed or roll-forward partitioning), whenever possible.[10] On the basis of these out-of-sample predictions, you might choose the best model (or an average of the better models) for forecasts of the future. Indeed, we can see from Table 5.5 that the manually selected AAM model outperforms the automatically selected MNA model when we compare their RMSEs in the validation set.

[10] Automation is inevitable in applications that require forecasting many series.

5.7 Extensions of Exponential Smoothing

Multiple Seasonal Cycles

Recently, the Holt-Winter's exponential smoothing method was extended to handle more than a single seasonal cycle. This is useful, for instance, when the series contains daily and monthly

```
ets.opt <- ets(train.ts)
ets.opt.pred <- forecast(ets.opt, h = nValid, level = 0)

> accuracy(hw.pred, valid.ts)
                ME     RMSE      MAE       MPE     MAPE      MASE
Training set 3.768926 56.91329 44.58956 0.1590906 2.538990 0.5405321
Test set     32.255818 82.18213 66.73520 1.5569775 3.390749 0.8089903
> accuracy(ets.opt.pred, valid.ts)
                ME     RMSE      MAE        MPE     MAPE      MASE
Training set 0.6435028 55.94998 44.36831 -0.04638523 2.528594 0.5378501
Test set     49.1800869 88.24383 73.51254  2.36734303 3.688069 0.8911478
```

Table 5.5: Comparison of manual and automated model selection, applied to the Amtrak ridership data.

seasonality, or hourly and daily seasonality. One example is electricity demand, which often exhibits a day-of-week cycle as well as a within-day cycle. Other examples include call center arrivals where operating hours differ on weekdays and week-ends[11], hospital admissions, and transportation and internet traffic.

The general idea behind the different proposed methods is adding a fourth component to the series, which reflects the second seasonal cycle. The second seasonal cycle appears in the formula for a k-step-ahead forecast and adds a fourth updating equation.

While there are several approaches, the basic double-seasonal model (with additive trend and multiplicative seasonality) by Taylor (2003) [12] uses four updating equations, one for each of four components: level, trend, cycle 1, and cycle 2. Using our previous notation, and assuming M_1 seasons (e.g., days) and M_2 sub-seasons (e.g., hours), k-step-ahead forecasts are given by the formula

$$F_{t+k} = (L_t + kT_t) \times S^{(1)}_{t+k-M_1} \times S^{(2)}_{t+k-M_2} \qquad (5.23)$$

with the four updating equations (and four corresponding smoothing constants $\alpha, \beta, \gamma_1, \gamma_2$):

$$L_t = \alpha Y_t / (S^{(1)}_{t-M_1} S^{(2)}_{t-M_2}) + (1 - \alpha)(L_{t-1} + T_{t-1}) \qquad (5.24)$$
$$T_t = \beta(L_t - L_{t-1}) + (1 - \beta)T_{t-1} \qquad (5.25)$$
$$S^{(1)}_t = \gamma_1 \left(y_t / (L_t S^{(2)}_{t-M2}) \right) + (1 - \gamma_1) S^{(1)}_{t-M_1} \qquad (5.26)$$

[11] J. W. Taylor and R. D. Snyder. Forecasting intraday time series with multiple seasonal cycles using parsimonious seasonal exponential smoothing. *Omega*, forthcoming, 2011

[12] J. W. Taylor. Exponentially weighted methods for forecasting intraday time series with multiple seasonal cycles. *International Journal of Forecasting*, 26:627–646, 2003

$$S_t^{(2)} = \gamma_2 \left(y_t / (L_t S_{t-M1}^{(1)}) \right) + (1 - \gamma_2) S_{t-M_2}^{(2)} \qquad (5.27)$$

This approach can be further extended to more than two seasonal cycles (such as hourly, daily, and monthly cycles). The *forecast* package in R includes the function dshw, which implements the double-seasonal Holt-Winter's method by Taylor (2003).

Adaptive Smoothing Constants

The smoothing constants or parameters (α, β, γ) in exponential smoothing are fixed (hence the term "constants"), so that their value does not change over time. There have been several attempts to incorporate time-varying smoothing constants, to allow even more flexibility of the exponential smoothing algorithm to adapt to changes in the characteristics of the time series over time.

One example is the "smooth transition exponential smoothing" (STES) approach by Taylor (2004) [13] where the smoothing constant for simple exponential smoothing is given by the logit function (which is restricted to the range 0-1)

$$\alpha_t = \frac{1}{1 + exp\{a + bV_t\}} \qquad (5.28)$$

where V_t is a user-specified transition variable, which "is of crucial importance to the success of the method" (Taylor suggests using the square or the absolute value of the forecast error from the most recent period). The parameters a, b are estimated from the training period.

Reported empirical performance of the various proposed methods shows mixed and sometimes contradictory results: while in some cases forecast accuracy is improved, in other series it is dramatically decreased. For more information, see Gardner (2006).[14]

[13] J. W. Taylor. Smooth transition exponential smoothing. *Journal of Forecasting*, 23:385–394, 2004

[14] E. J. Gardner. Exponential smoothing: The state of the art - Part II. *International Journal of Forecasting*, 22:637–666, 2006

5.8 Problems

1. *Impact of September 11 on Air Travel in the United States:* The Research and Innovative Technology Administration's Bureau of Transportation Statistics (BTS) conducted a study to evaluate the impact of the September 11, 2001, terrorist attack on U.S. transportation. The study report and the data can be found at `www.bts.gov/publications/estimated_impacts_of_9_11_on_us_travel`. The goal of the study was stated as follows:

Figure 5.7: Air travel. (Image by africa / FreeDigitalPhotos.net)

> The purpose of this study is to provide a greater understanding of the passenger travel behavior patterns of persons making long distance trips before and after September 11.

The report analyzes monthly passenger movement data between January 1990 and April 2004. Data on three monthly time series are given in the file *Sept11Travel.xls* for this period: (1) actual airline revenue passenger miles (Air), (2) rail passenger miles (Rail), and (3) vehicle miles traveled (Auto).

In order to assess the impact of September 11, BTS took the following approach: Using data before September 11, it forecasted future data (under the assumption of no terrorist attack). Then, BTS compared the forecasted series with the actual data to assess the impact of the event. Our first step, therefore, is to split each of the time series into two parts: pre- and post-September 11. We now concentrate only on the earlier time series.

(a) Create a time plot for the pre-event Air time series. What time series components appear from the plot?

(b) Figure 5.8 below is a time plot of the seasonally adjusted pre-September-11 Air series. Which of the following smoothing methods would be adequate for forecasting this series?

- Naive forecasts
- Moving average (with what window width?)
- Simple exponential smoothing
- Double exponential smoothing
- Holt-Winter's exponential smoothing

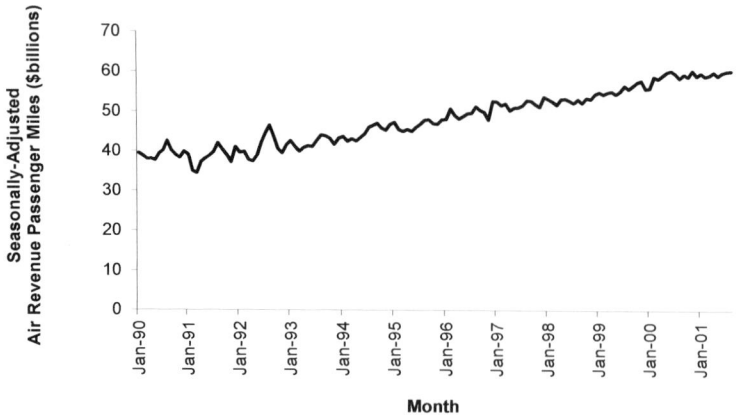

Figure 5.8: Seasonally adjusted pre-September-11 air series

2. *Relation between Moving Average and Exponential Smoothing:* Assume that we apply a moving average to a series, using a very short window span. If we wanted to achieve an equivalent result using simple exponential smoothing, what value should the smoothing coefficient take?

3. *Forecasting with a Moving Average:* For a given time series of sales, the training period consists of 50 months. The first 5 months' data are shown below:

Month	Sales
Sept 98	27
Oct 98	31
Nov 98	58
Dec 98	63
Jan 99	59

(a) Compute the sales forecast for January 1999 based on a moving average model with span $w = 4$.

(b) Compute the forecast error for the above forecast

4. *Optimizing Exponential Smoothing:* The table below shows the optimal smoothing constants from applying exponential smoothing to data, using automated model selection:

Level	1.000
Trend	0.000
Seasonality	0.246

(a) Using a series partitioned into training/validation periods and the ets function in R, the optimized smoothing constants are those that minimize (choose one of the following):

- The MAPE over the training period
- The MAPE over the validation period
- The RMSE over the training period
- The RMSE over the validation period
- Fit to the training period with a penalty on the number of parameters
- Fit to the validation period with a penalty on the number of parameters

(b) The value of zero that is obtained for the trend smoothing constant means that (choose one of the following):

- There is no trend
- The trend is estimated only from the first two points
- The trend is updated throughout the data
- The trend is statistically insignificant

(c) What is the danger of using the optimal smoothing constant values?

5. *Forecasting Department Store Sales:* The file *DepartmentStore-Sales.xls* contains data on the quarterly sales for a department store over a 6-year period (data courtesy of Chris Albright).

The time plot of the data is shown in Figure 5.10.

Figure 5.9: (Image by Paul Martin Eldridge / FreeDigitalPhotos.net)

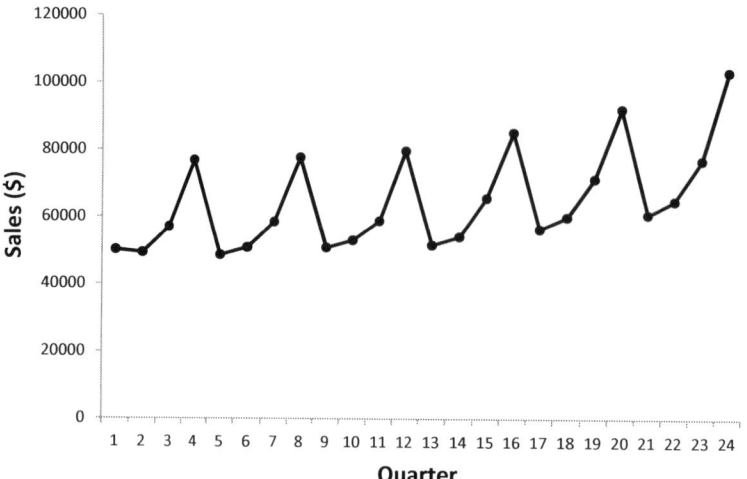

Figure 5.10: Department store quarterly sales series

(a) Which of the following methods would not be suitable for forecasting this series?

- Moving average of raw series
- Moving average of deseasonalized series
- Simple exponential smoothing of the raw series
- Double exponential smoothing of the raw series
- Holt-Winter's exponential smoothing of the raw series

(b) A forecaster was tasked to generate forecasts for 4 quarters ahead. She therefore partitioned the data so that the last 4 quarters were designated as the validation period. The forecaster approached the forecasting task by using multiplicative Holt-Winter's exponential smoothing. The smoothing constants used were $\alpha = 0.2, \beta = 0.15, \gamma = 0.05$.

i. Run this method on the data. Request the forecasts on the validation period.

ii. The Holt-Winter's forecasts for the validation set are given in Table 5.6. Compute the MAPE values for the forecasts of quarters 21-22.

Quarter	Actual	Forecast	Error
21	60800	59384.56586	1415.434145
22	64900	61656.49426	3243.505741
23	76997	71853.01442	5143.985579
24	103337	95074.69842	8262.301585

Table 5.6: Forecasts for validation series using exponential smoothing

(c) The fit and residuals are displayed in Figure 5.11. Using all the information from (b) and (c), is this model suitable for forecasting quarters 21 and 22?

Figure 5.11: Forecasts and forecast errors using regression (left) and exponential smoothing (right)

(d) Another analyst decided to take a much simpler approach, and instead of using exponential smoothing he used differencing. Use differencing to remove the trend and seasonal pattern. Which order works better: first removing trend and then seasonality or the opposite order? Show a time plot of your final series.

(e) Forecast quarters 21-22 using the average of the double-differenced series from (d). Remember to use only the training period (until quarter 20), and to adjust back for the trend and seasonal pattern.

(f) Compare the forecasts from (e) to the exponential smoothing forecasts in the table in (b). Which of the two forecasting methods would you choose? Explain.

(g) What is an even simpler approach that should be compared as a baseline?

6. *Shipments of Household Appliances:* The file *ApplianceShipments.xls* contains the series of quarterly shipments (in millions of USD) of U.S. household appliances between 1985 and 1989 (data courtesy of Ken Black). A time plot of the data is shown in Figure 5.12.

Figure 5.12: Quarterly shipments of U.S. household appliances over 5 years

(a) Which of the following methods would be suitable for forecasting this series if applied to the raw data?

   • Naive forecasts

- Moving average
- Simple exponential smoothing
- Double exponential smoothing
- Holt-Winter's exponential smoothing

(b) Apply a moving average with window span $w = 4$ to the data. Use all but that last year as the training period. Create a time plot of the moving average series.

    i. What does the MA(4) chart reveal?

    ii. Use the MA(4) model to forecast appliance sales in Q1-1990.

    iii. Use the MA(4) model to forecast appliance sales in Q1-1991.

    iv. Is the Q1-1990 forecast most likely to underestimate, overestimate, or accurately estimate the actual sales on Q1-1990? Explain.

    v. Management feels most comfortable with moving averages. The analyst therefore plans to use this method for forecasting future quarters. What else should be considered before using the MA(4) to forecast future quarterly shipments of household appliances?

(c) We now focus on forecasting beyond 1989. In the following, continue to use all but the last year as the training period and the last four quarters as the validation period. Apply Holt-Winter's exponential smoothing to the training period.

    i. Compute the MAPE for the validation period using Holt-Winter's exponential smoothing.

    ii. Compare the MA(4) and Holt-Winter's results. Which model would you prefer to use for forecasting Q1-1990? Give three reasons.

7. *Forecasting Shampoo Sales:* The time series plot in Figure 5.13 below describes monthly sales of a certain shampoo over a 3-year period. Data available in *ShampooSales.xls* [source: Hyndman, R. J. Time Series Data Library, http://data.is/ TSDLdemo; accessed on July 13, 2015.]

Figure 5.13: Monthly sales of shampoo over 3 years

Which of the following methods would be suitable for forecasting this series if applied to the raw data?

- Moving average

- Simple exponential smoothing

- Double exponential smoothing

- Holt-Winter's exponential smoothing

8. *Forecasting Australian Wine Sales:* Figure 5.15 shows time plots of monthly sales of six types of Australian wines (red, rose, sweet white, dry white, sparkling, and fortified) for 1980-1994. Data available in *AustralianWines.xls* [source: Hyndman, R. J. Time Series Data Library, `http://data.is/TSDLdemo`; accessed on July 13, 2015.] The units are thousands of liters. You are hired to obtain short-term forecasts (2-3 months ahead) for each of the six series, and this task will be repeated every month.

Figure 5.14: (Image by Naypong / FreeDigitalPhotos.net)

(a) Which smoothing method would you choose if you had to choose the same method for forecasting all series? Why?

(b) Fortified wine has the largest market share of the six types of wine. You are asked to focus on fortified wine sales alone and produce as accurate a forecast as possible for the next two months.

Sweet Wine Sales

Rose Wine Sales

Sparkling Wine Sales

Red Wine Sales

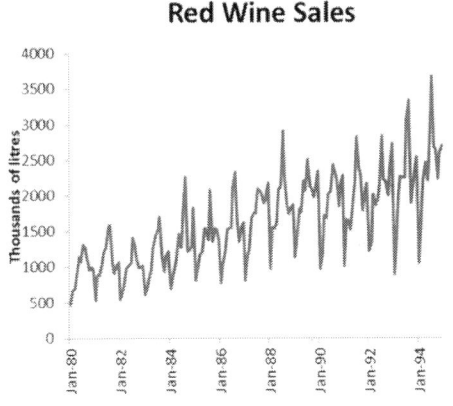

Dry White Wine Sales

Fortified Wine Sales

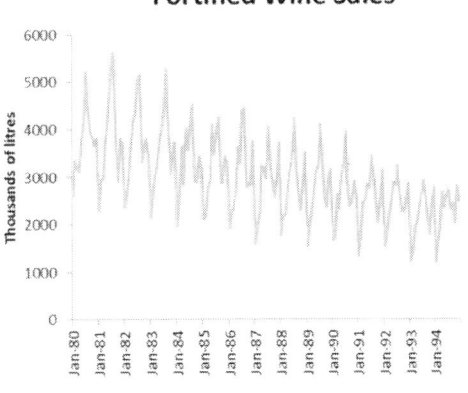

Figure 5.15: Monthly sales of six types of Australian wines between 1980-1994

- Start by partitioning the data using the period until Dec-1993 as the training period.
- Apply Holt-Winter's exponential smoothing (with multiplicative seasonality) to sales.

(c) Create a plot for the residuals from the Holt-Winter's exponential smoothing.

  i. Based on this plot, which of the following statements are reasonable?

  - Decembers (month 12) are not captured well by the model.
  - There is a strong correlation between sales on the same calendar month.
  - The model does not capture the seasonality well.
  - We should first deseasonalize the data and then apply Holt-Winter's exponential smoothing.

  ii. How can you handle the above effect with exponential smoothing?

9. *Natural Gas Sales:* Figure 5.16 shows a time plot of quarterly natural gas sales (in billions of BTU's) of a certain company, over a period of 4 years. (Data courtesy of George McCabe.) The company's analyst is asked to use a moving average model to forecast sales in Winter 2005.

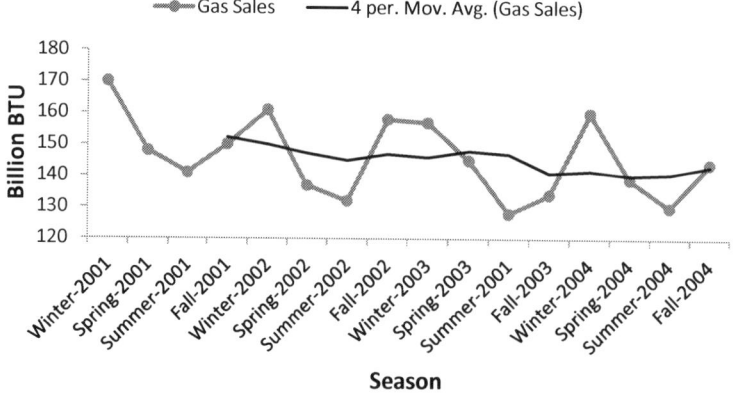

Figure 5.16: Quarterly sales of natural gas over 4 years

(a) Reproduce the time plot with the overlaying MA(4) line.

(b) What can we learn about the series from the MA line?

(c) Run a moving average forecaster with adequate season length. Are forecasts generated by this method expected to over-forecast, under-forecast, or accurately forecast actual sales? Why?

6
Regression-Based Models

A popular forecasting tool is based on *linear regression* models, using suitable predictors to capture trend and/or seasonality as well as other patterns. In this chapter, we show how a linear regression model can be set up to capture a time series with a trend and/or seasonality. The model, which is estimated from the training period, can then produce forecasts on future data by inserting the relevant predictor information into the estimated regression equation. We describe different types of common trends (linear, exponential, polynomial, etc.), as well as two types of seasonality (additive and multiplicative) and the use of a sine and cosine terms.

After discussing trend and seasonality, we show how a regression model can be used to quantify the correlation between neighboring values in a time series (called *autocorrelation*). This type of model, called an *autoregressive* (AR) model, is useful for improving forecast accuracy by making use of the information contained in the autocorrelation (beyond trend and seasonality). It is also useful for evaluating the predictability of a series (by evaluating whether the series is a "random walk"). The various steps of fitting linear regression and autoregressive models, using them to generate forecasts, and assessing their predictive accuracy, are illustrated using the Amtrak ridership series.

6.1   Model with Trend

Linear regression can be used to fit a global trend that applies to the entire series and will apply in the forecasting period. A linear trend means that the values of the series increase or decrease linearly in time, whereas an exponential trend captures an exponential increase or decrease. We can also use more flexible functions, such a quadratic functions or higher order polynomials, to capture more complex trend shapes. In the following sections we will discuss each of several common trend types and how to set up the linear regression accordingly.

Linear Trend

To create a linear regression model that captures a time series with a global linear trend, the output variable (y) is set as the time series measurement or some function of it, and the predictor (x) is set as a time index. Let us consider a simple example: fitting a linear trend to the Amtrak ridership data. The first step is to create a new column that is a time index $t = 1, 2, 3, \ldots$ This will serve as our predictor. A snapshot of the two corresponding columns (y and t) in Excel is shown in Figure 6.1.

Month	Ridership	t
Jan-91	1709	1
Feb-91	1621	2
Mar-91	1973	3
Apr-91	1812	4
May-91	1975	5
Jun-91	1862	6
Jul-91	1940	7
Aug-91	2013	8
Sep-91	1596	9
Oct-91	1725	10
Nov-91	1676	11
Dec-91	1814	12
Jan-92	1615	13
Feb-92	1557	14

Figure 6.1: Output variable (middle) and predictor variable (right) used to fit a linear trend

Before fitting the linear regression, we partition the ridership time series into training and validation periods, so that the last year of data (Apr 2003 to March 2004) is the validation period. Reasons for keeping 12 months in the validation set are (1) if the purpose is to provide monthly forecasts for the year ahead, and (2) to allow evaluation of forecasts on different months of the year.

A linear trend fitted to the training period is shown in Figure 6.2. From the time plot it is obvious that the global trend of the series is not linear. However, we use this example to illustrate how a linear trend is fit, and later we consider other models for this series.

To fit a linear relationship between *Ridership* and *Time*, we set the output variable y as the Amtrak ridership and the predictor as the time index t in the regression model:

$$y_t = \beta_0 + \beta_1 t + \epsilon \qquad (6.1)$$

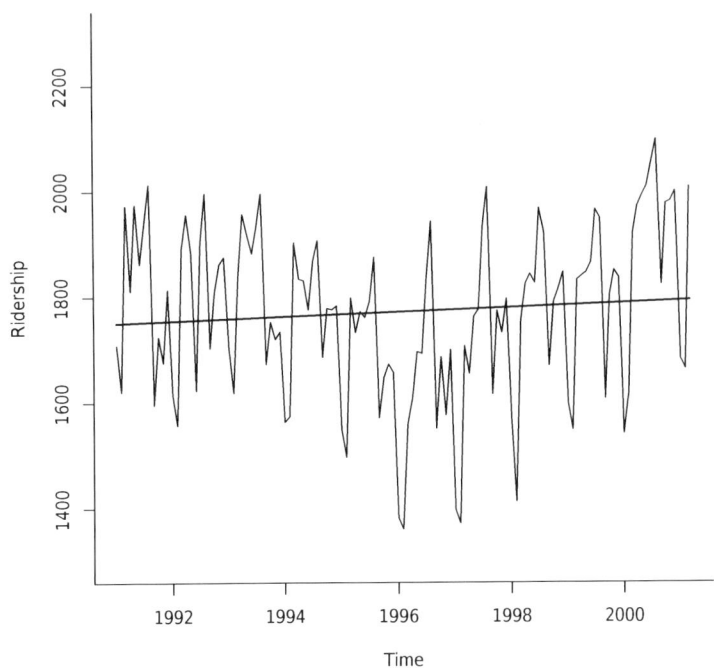

Figure 6.2: Linear trend fitted to the Amtrak ridership data.

 code for creating Figure 6.2

```
train.lm <- tslm(train.ts ~ trend)

plot(train.ts, xlab = "Time", ylab = "Ridership", ylim = c(1300, 2300), bty = "l")
lines(train.lm$fitted, lwd = 2)
```

Use the tslm function (which stands for time series linear model) with the formula train.ts ~ trend to produce a linear trend model. Plot the time series and the linear trend model's fitted values.

where y_t is the Ridership at time point t and ϵ is the standard noise term in a linear regression. Thus, we are modeling three of the four time series components: level (β_0), trend (β_1), and noise (ϵ). Seasonality is not modeled.

The next step is to use the linear trend model (also a linear regression model) to make forecasts in the validation period. Figure 6.3 depicts the fitted linear model and its predictions in the validation period.

The linear trend model in Figure 6.3 is also a linear regression model. Table 6.1 presents the model's summary output from R.

```
> summary(train.lm)

Call: lm(formula = formula, data = "train.ts", na.action = na.exclude)

Residuals:
    Min      1Q  Median      3Q     Max
-411.29 -114.02   16.06  129.28  306.35

Coefficients:
            Estimate Std. Error t value Pr(>|t|)
(Intercept) 1750.3595    29.0729  60.206   <2e-16 ***
trend          0.3514     0.4069   0.864     0.39
---
Signif. codes:  0 *** 0.001 ** 0.01 * 0.05 . 0.1   1

Residual standard error: 160.2 on 121 degrees of freedom
Multiple R-squared:  0.006125,        Adjusted R-squared:  -0.002089
F-statistic: 0.7456 on 1 and 121 DF,  p-value: 0.3896
```

Table 6.1: Summary of output from a linear regression model applied to the Amtrak ridership data in the training period.

Note: beware of examining only the estimated coefficients and their statistical significance for making decisions about the trend, as this can be misleading. A significant coefficient for trend does not mean that a linear fit is adequate. An insignificant coefficient does not mean that there is no trend in the data. In our example, the slope coefficient (0.3514) is insignificant (p-value=0.39), yet there may be a trend in the data (often once we control for seasonality). For instance, when we run a linear regression on the deseasonalized Amtrak ridership data in the top right of Figure 5.4, we find the trend coefficient (0.8294) is statistically significant (p-value<0.001). To determine suitability

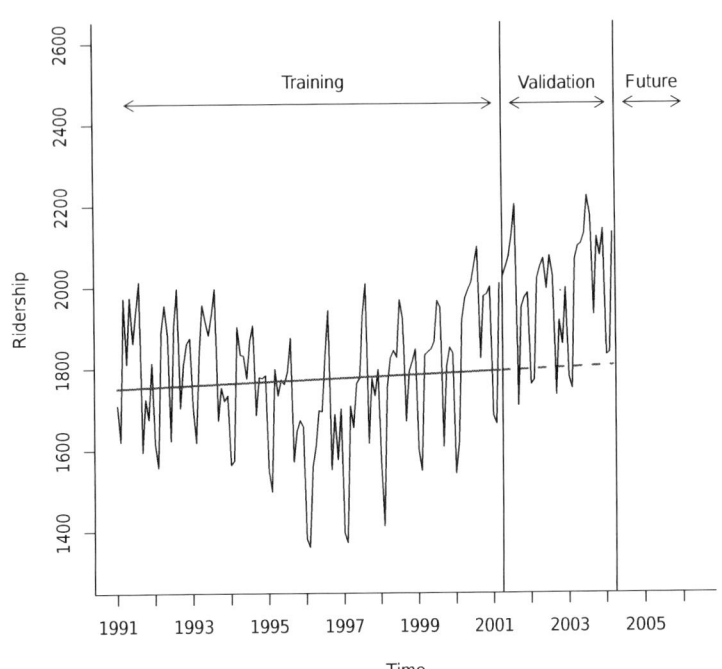

Figure 6.3: Linear trend fitted to the Amtrak ridership data in the training period and forecasted in the validation period.

 code for creating Figure 6.3

```
train.lm.pred <- forecast(train.lm, h = nValid, level = 0)

plot(train.lm.pred, ylim = c(1300, 2600),  ylab = "Ridership", xlab = "Time",
    bty = "l", xaxt = "n", xlim = c(1991,2006.25), main = "", flty = 2)
axis(1, at = seq(1991, 2006, 1), labels = format(seq(1991, 2006, 1)))
lines(train.lm.pred$fitted, lwd = 2, col = "blue")
lines(valid.ts)
```

of any trend shape, look at the time plot of the (deseasonalized) time series with the trend overlaid; examine the residual time plot; and look at performance measures on the validation period.

Exponential Trend

There are several alternative trend shapes that are useful and easy to fit via a linear regression model. One such shape is an exponential trend. An exponential trend implies a multiplicative increase/decrease of the series over time ($y_t = ce^{\beta_1 t + \epsilon}$).

To fit an exponential trend, simply replace the output variable y with $\log(y)$ and fit a linear regression[1]:

$$\log(y_t) = \beta_0 + \beta_1 t + \epsilon \tag{6.2}$$

In the Amtrak example, for instance, we would fit a linear regression of *log(Ridership)* on the index variable t. Exponential trends are popular in sales data, where they reflect percentage growth.

Note: As in the general case of linear regression, when comparing the predictive accuracy of models that have a different output variable, such as a linear model trend (with y) and an exponential model trend (with $\log(y)$), it is essential to compare forecast or forecast errors on the same scale. An exponential trend model will produce forecasts in logarithmic scale, and the forecast errors reported by many software packages will therefore be of the form $\log(y_t) - F_t$.

In R, the process of obtaining forecasts in the original scale is automated. Figure 6.5 shows the predictions from a linear regression model fit to *log(Ridership)*. The linear trend model is overlaid on top of this exponential trend model. The two trends do not appear to be very different because the time horizon is short and the increase is gentle.

Polynomial Trend

Another nonlinear trend shape that is easy to fit via linear regression is a polynomial trend, and in particular, a quadratic

[1] We use "log" to denote the natural logarithm (base e). In Excel this is computed using the function =*ln*.

Figure 6.4: An exponential trend reflects percentage increase/decrease. (Image by Danilo Rizzuti / FreeDigitalPhotos.net)

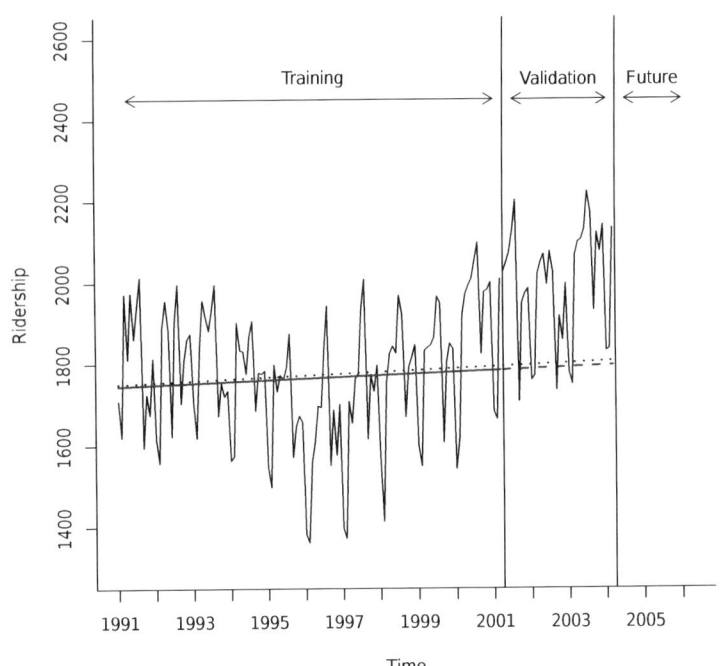

Figure 6.5: Exponential (and linear) trend fitted to the Amtrak ridership data in the training period and forecasted in the validation period. The exponential trend is the solid line in the training period and the long-dashed line in the validation period. The linear trend is the short-dashed line.

 code for creating Figure 6.3

```
train.lm.expo.trend <- tslm(train.ts ~ trend, lambda = 0)
train.lm.expo.trend.pred <- forecast(train.lm.expo.trend, h = nValid, level = 0)

train.lm.linear.trend <- tslm(train.ts ~ trend, lambda = 1)
train.lm.linear.trend.pred <- forecast(train.lm.linear.trend, h = nValid, level = 0)

plot(train.lm.expo.trend.pred, ylim = c(1300, 2600),  ylab = "Ridership", xlab = "Time", bty = "l",
    xaxt = "n", xlim = c(1991,2006.25), main = "", flty = 2)
axis(1, at = seq(1991, 2006, 1), labels = format(seq(1991, 2006, 1)))
lines(train.lm.expo.trend.pred$fitted, lwd = 2, col = "blue")
lines(train.lm.linear.trend.pred$fitted, lwd = 2, col = "black", lty = 3)
lines(train.lm.linear.trend.pred$mean, lwd = 2, col = "black", lty = 3)
lines(valid.ts)
```

Use the tslm function again, but with the argument lambda = 0. With this argument included, the tslm function applies the Box-Cox transformation to the ridership data in the training period. The Box-Cox transformation is $(y^\lambda - 1)/\lambda$ if $\lambda \neq 0$. For $\lambda = 0$, the transformation is defined as $\log(y)$—BoxCox(train.ts, 0) in R. Note that with $\lambda = 1$, the series is not transformed (except for the subtraction of 1 from each point), and the regression model fit will have a linear trend. When generating forecasts from a model with $\lambda \neq 1$, the forecast function automatically converts the model's predictions back into the original scale.

relationship of the form

$$y_t = \beta_0 + \beta_1 t + \beta_2 t^2 + \epsilon. \qquad (6.3)$$

This is done by creating an additional predictor t^2 (the square of t) and fitting a multiple linear regression with the two predictors t and t^2. For the Amtrak ridership data, we have already seen a U-shaped trend in the data. We therefore fit a quadratic model to the training period. See the output in Table 6.2.

Table 6.2: Summary of output from fitting a quadratic trend to the Amtrak ridership data in the training period.

```
> train.lm.poly.trend <- tslm(train.ts ~ poly(trend, 2, raw = TRUE))
> summary(train.lm.poly.trend)

Call:
lm(formula = formula, data = "train.ts", na.action = na.exclude)

Residuals:
    Min      1Q  Median      3Q     Max
-344.79 -101.86   40.89   98.54  279.81

Coefficients:
                            Estimate Std. Error t value Pr(>|t|)
(Intercept)               1888.88401   40.91521  46.166  < 2e-16 ***
poly(trend, 2, raw = TRUE)1 -6.29780    1.52327  -4.134 6.63e-05 ***
poly(trend, 2, raw = TRUE)2  0.05362    0.01190   4.506 1.55e-05 ***
---
Signif. codes:  0 *** 0.001 ** 0.01 * 0.05 . 0.1   1

Residual standard error: 148.8 on 120 degrees of freedom
Multiple R-squared:  0.1499,        Adjusted R-squared:  0.1358
F-statistic: 10.58 on 2 and 120 DF,  p-value: 5.844e-05
```

Note that we must include the argument raw = TRUE in the poly function in order to get the proper coefficients and statistics in the summary. You can use the call train.lm.poly.trend$data in R to see the raw data the regression uses. The quadratic equation fit by the tslm function is $1888.88401 - 6.29780t + 0.05362t^2$ where t (or trend) goes from 1 to 123 in the training period and from 124 to 159 in the validation period. Another way to fit a quadratic trend is with tslm(train.ts ~ trend + I(trend^2). The function I treats an object "as is".

From the plot of the quadratic fit (Figure 3.2, back in Chapter 3), we can see that this shape captures the pattern in the trend in the training period. The residuals (shown in Figure 3.3) now exhibit only seasonality. In general, any type of trend shape can be fit as long as it has a mathematical representation. However, the underlying assumption is that this shape is applicable throughout the period of data that we currently have as well as during the validation period and future. Do not choose an overly complex shape, because although it will fit the training period well, it will likely be overfitting the data. To avoid overfitting, always examine performance on the validation period and refrain from choosing overly complex trend patterns.

6.2 Model with Seasonality

A seasonal pattern in a time series means that observations that fall in some seasons have consistently higher or lower values than those that fall in other seasons. Examples are day-of-week patterns, monthly patterns, and quarterly patterns. The Amtrak ridership monthly time series, as can be seen in the time plot, exhibits strong monthly seasonality (with highest traffic during summer months).

The most common way to capture seasonality in a regression model is by creating a new categorical variable that denotes the season for each observation. This categorical variable is then turned into dummy variables, which in turn are included as predictors in the regression model. To illustrate this, we created a new Month column for the Amtrak ridership data, as shown in Figure 6.6.

In order to include the season categorical variable as a predictor in a regression model for y (e.g., Ridership), we turn it into dummy variables. For m seasons we create $m - 1$ dummy variables, which are binary variables that take on the value 1 if the record falls in that particular season, and 0 otherwise. The mth season does not require a dummy, since it is identified when all the $m - 1$ dummies take on zero values.

Table 6.3 shows the output of a linear regression fit to Ridership (y) on 11-month dummy variables (using the training

Month	Ridership	Season
Jan-91	1709	Jan
Feb-91	1621	Feb
Mar-91	1973	Mar
Apr-91	1812	Apr
May-91	1975	May
Jun-91	1862	Jun
Jul-91	1940	Jul
Aug-91	2013	Aug
Sep-91	1596	Sep
Oct-91	1725	Oct
Nov-91	1676	Nov
Dec-91	1814	Dec
Jan-92	1615	Jan
Feb-92	1557	Feb
Mar-92	1891	Mar
Apr-92	1956	Apr
May-92	1885	May

Figure 6.6: New categorical variable "Season" (right) to be used (via dummy variables) as predictor(s) in a linear regression model

period). The fitted series and the residuals from this model are shown in Figure 6.7. The model appears to capture the seasonality in the data. However, since we have not included a trend component in the model (as shown in Section 6.1), the fitted values do not capture the existing trend, as evident by the three months with "dips" in the middle of the series and the months with peaks at the end of the series. Therefore, the residuals, which are the difference between the actual and fitted values, clearly display the remaining U-shaped trend. During the middle period, the series is over-predicted, while the start and end of the series are under-predicted.

When seasonality is added as described above (create a categorical seasonal variable, then create dummy variables from it, and then regress on y), it captures *additive seasonality*. This means that the average value of y in a certain season is higher or lower by a fixed amount compared to another season. For example, in the Amtrak ridership, the coefficient for August (396.66) indicates that the average number of passengers in August is higher by 396,660 passengers compared to the average in January (the reference category). Using regression models, we can also capture *multiplicative seasonality*, where average values on a certain season are higher or lower by a fixed percentage compared to another season. To fit multiplicative seasonality, we use the same model as above, except that we use $\log(y)$ as the output variable.[2]

[2] To do this in R, we include the argument `lambda = 0` in the `tslm` call.

Table 6.3: Summary of output from fitting a quadratic trend to the Amtrak ridership data in the training period.

```
> train.lm.season <- tslm(train.ts ~ season)
> summary(train.lm.season)

Call:
lm(formula = formula, data = "train.ts", na.action = na.exclude)

Residuals:
     Min      1Q   Median      3Q     Max
-276.165  -52.934    5.868  54.544  215.081

Coefficients:
            Estimate Std. Error t value Pr(>|t|)
(Intercept)  1573.97      30.58  51.475  < 2e-16 ***
season2       -42.93      43.24  -0.993   0.3230
season3       260.77      43.24   6.030 2.19e-08 ***
season4       245.09      44.31   5.531 2.14e-07 ***
season5       278.22      44.31   6.279 6.81e-09 ***
season6       233.46      44.31   5.269 6.82e-07 ***
season7       345.33      44.31   7.793 3.79e-12 ***
season8       396.66      44.31   8.952 9.19e-15 ***
season9        75.76      44.31   1.710   0.0901 .
season10      200.61      44.31   4.527 1.51e-05 ***
season11      192.36      44.31   4.341 3.14e-05 ***
season12      230.42      44.31   5.200 9.18e-07 ***
---
Signif. codes:  0 *** 0.001 ** 0.01 * 0.05 . 0.1   1

Residual standard error: 101.4 on 111 degrees of freedom
Multiple R-squared:  0.6348,     Adjusted R-squared:  0.5986
F-statistic: 17.54 on 11 and 111 DF,  p-value: < 2.2e-16
```

We include season as a predictor in the tslm function. This predictor is actually 11 dummy variables, one for each season—except for the first season, January. If you ever forget which season is season1, run the line train.lm.season$data to see which season number goes with which month (or day or hour).

Figure 6.7: Regression model with seasonality fitted to the Amtrak ridership data in the top panel (model is thick training line and broken validation line). The model's residuals are in the bottom panel.

6.3 Model with Trend and Seasonality

We can create models that capture both trend and seasonality by including predictors of both types. Our exploration of the Amtrak ridership data indicates that a quadratic trend and monthly seasonality are both warranted. We therefore fit a model with 13 predictors: 11 dummy variables for month, and t and t^2 for trend. The output for this final model is in Table 6.4. The model's fit and residuals are depict in Figure 6.8.

```
> train.lm.trend.season <- tslm(train.ts ~ trend + I(trend^2) + season)
> summary(train.lm.trend.season)

Call:
lm(formula = formula, data = "train.ts", na.action = na.exclude)

Residuals:
     Min       1Q   Median       3Q      Max
-213.775  -39.363    9.711   42.422  152.187

Coefficients:
              Estimate Std. Error t value Pr(>|t|)
(Intercept)  1.697e+03  2.768e+01  61.318  < 2e-16 ***
trend       -7.156e+00  7.293e-01  -9.812  < 2e-16 ***
I(trend^2)   6.074e-02  5.698e-03  10.660  < 2e-16 ***
season2     -4.325e+01  3.024e+01  -1.430  0.15556
season3      2.600e+02  3.024e+01   8.598 6.60e-14 ***
season4      2.606e+02  3.102e+01   8.401 1.83e-13 ***
season5      2.938e+02  3.102e+01   9.471 6.89e-16 ***
season6      2.490e+02  3.102e+01   8.026 1.26e-12 ***
season7      3.606e+02  3.102e+01  11.626  < 2e-16 ***
season8      4.117e+02  3.102e+01  13.270  < 2e-16 ***
season9      9.032e+01  3.102e+01   2.911  0.00437 **
season10     2.146e+02  3.102e+01   6.917 3.29e-10 ***
season11     2.057e+02  3.103e+01   6.629 1.34e-09 ***
season12     2.429e+02  3.103e+01   7.829 3.44e-12 ***
---
Signif. codes:  0 *** 0.001 ** 0.01 * 0.05 . 0.1   1

Residual standard error: 70.92 on 109 degrees of freedom
Multiple R-squared:  0.8246,        Adjusted R-squared:  0.8037
F-statistic: 39.42 on 13 and 109 DF,  p-value: < 2.2e-16
```

Table 6.4: Summary of output from fitting model with quadratic trend and seasonality to the Amtrak ridership data in the training period.

Figure 6.8: Regression model with quadratic trend and seasonality fitted to the Amtrak ridership data in the top panel. The model's residuals are in the bottom panel.

After exploring different regression models and choosing the model to be used for forecasting, we refit the chosen regression model to the recombined training and validation periods. Then, the model can be used to generate k-step-ahead forecasts, denoted F_{t+k} (see Section 1.4).

When a continuous mathematical function can approximate the seasonal pattern, we can use approximations such as sinusoidal functions as predictors in the regression model. For example, the Centers for Disease Control and Prevention in the United States use a regression model for modeling the percent of weekly deaths attributed to pneumonia & influenza in 122 cities. The model includes a quadrtic trend as well as sine and cosine functions for capturing the smooth seasonality pattern.[3] In particular, they use the following regression model:

[3] See www.cdc.gov/mmwr/ preview/mmwrhtml/ mm5914a3.htm.

$$y_t = \beta_0 + \beta_1 t + \beta_2 t^2 + \beta_3 \sin(2\pi t/52.18) + \beta_4 \cos(2\pi t/52.18) + \epsilon$$
$$(6.4)$$

The trend terms t and t^2 accommodate long-term linear and

Figure 6.9: Regression model (lower smooth line) for weekly deaths attributed to penumonia & influenza. From www.cdc.gov

curvilinear changes in the background proportion of pneumonia & influenza deaths arising from factors such as population growth or improved disease prevention or treatment. The sine and cosine terms capture the yearly periodicity of weekly data (with 52.18 weeks per year).[4] This regression model is then fitted to five years of data to create a "baseline" against which new

[4] To capture the same type of pattern with daily data, one can use $\sin(2\pi t/365.25)$ and $\cos(2\pi t/365.25)$.

weekly mortality is compared, called the 'Serfling method' (see Figure 6.9).

For more on the use of forecasting in early disease detection, see the article by Burkom et al. (2007).[5]

To fit a model with linear, quadratic, sine, and cosine terms to the Amtrak ridership data in R, we add three additional predictors to the linear trend model in Figure 6.2, as shown in Table 6.5.

[5] H. S. Burkom, S. P. Murphy, and G. Shmueli. Automated time series forecasting for biosurveillance. *Statistics in Medicine*, 26:4202–4218, 2007

```
tslm(train.ts ~ trend + I(trend^2) + I(sin(2*pi*trend/12))
              + I(cos(2*pi*trend/12)))
```

Table 6.5: Model with linear, quadratic, sine, and cosine terms fit to the Amtrak ridership data in the training period.

6.4   *Autocorrelation and ARIMA Models*

When we use linear regression for time series forecasting, we are able to account for patterns such as trend and seasonality. However, ordinary regression models do not account for dependence between observations, which in cross-sectional data is assumed to be absent. Yet, in the time series context, observations in neighboring periods tend to be correlated. Such correlation, called *autocorrelation*, is informative and can help in improving forecasts. If we know that values tends to be followed by similar values (positive autocorrelation) or by very different values (negative autocorrelation), then we can use that information to adjust forecasts. We will now discuss how to compute the autocorrelation of a series and how best to utilize the information for improving forecasting.

Computing Autocorrelation

Correlation between values of a time series in neighboring periods is called *autocorrelation* because it describes a relationship between the series and itself. To compute autocorrelation, we compute the correlation between the series and a lagged version of the series. A lagged series is a "copy" of the original series, which is moved forward one or more time periods. A lagged series with lag-1 is the original series moved forward one time period; a lagged series with lag-2 is the original series moved forward two time periods, and so on. Figure 6.10 shows the first 24 months of the Amtrak ridership series, the lag-1 series and the lag-2 series.

	A	B	C	D	E
1	Month	Ridership	Lag 1 Series	Lag 2 Series	
2	Jan-91	1709			
3	Feb-91	1621	1709		
4	Mar-91	1973	1621	1709	
5	Apr-91	1812	1973	1621	
6	May-91	1975	1812	1973	
7	Jun-91	1862	1975	1812	
8	Jul-91	1940	1862	1975	
9	Aug-91	2013	1940	1862	
10	Sep-91	1596	2013	1940	
11	Oct-91	1725	1596	2013	
12	Nov-91	1676	1725	1596	
13	Dec-91	1814	1676	1725	
14	Jan-92	1615	1814	1676	
15	Feb-92	1557	1615	1814	
16	Mar-92	1891	1557	1615	
17	Apr-92	1956	1891	1557	
18	May-92	1885	1956	1891	
19	Jun-92	1623	1885	1956	
20	Jul-92	1903	1623	1885	
21	Aug-92	1997	1903	1623	
22	Sep-92	1704	1997	1903	
23	Oct-92	1810	1704	1997	
24	Nov-92	1862	1810	1704	
25	Dec-92	1875	1862	1810	
26					

Figure 6.10: First 24 months of Amtrak ridership series, lag-1 series, and lag-2 series

Next, to compute the lag-1 autocorrelation (which measures the linear relationship between values in consecutive time periods), we compute the correlation between the original series and the lag-1 series (e.g., via the Excel function CORREL) to be 0.08. Note that although the original series shown in Figure 6.10 has 24 time periods, the lag-1 autocorrelation will only be based on 23 pairs (because the lag-1 series does not have a value for Jan-91). Similarly, the lag-2 autocorrelation (measuring the relationship between values that are two time periods apart) is the correlation between the original series and the lag-2 series (yielding -0.15).

We can use the forecast package's Acf function to compute and plot the autocorrelations of a series at different lags (see Figure 6.11).

code for creating Figure 6.11

```
ridership.24.ts <- window(ridership.ts, start = c(1991, 1), end = c(1991, 24))
Acf(ridership.24.ts, lag.max = 12, main = "")
```

Figure 6.11: Acf output
showing autocorrelations
at lags 1-12 for the first 24
months of Amtrak ridership.

Strong autocorrelation (positive or negative) at a lag larger than
    1 typically reflects a cyclical pattern. For example, strong
    positive autocorrelation at lag-12 in monthly data will reflect
    an annual seasonality (where values during a given month
    each year are positively correlated).

Positive lag-1 autocorrelation (called "stickiness") describes a series
    where consecutive values move generally in the same direc-
    tion. In the presence of a strong linear trend, we would expect
    to see a strong and positive lag-1 autocorrelation.

Negative lag-1 autocorrelation reflects swings in the series, where
    high values are immediately followed by low values and vice
    versa.

Examining the autocorrelation of a series can therefore help to
detect seasonality patterns. In Figure 6.11, for example, we see
that the strongest autocorrelation is negative and at lag 6. This
indicates a biannual pattern in ridership, with 6-month switches
from high to low ridership. A look at the time plot confirms the
high-summer low-winter pattern.

In addition to looking at autocorrelations of the raw series, it
is very useful to look at autocorrelations of residual series. For
example, after fitting a regression model (or using any other
forecasting method), we can examine the autocorrelation of the
series of residuals. If we have adequately modeled the seasonal
pattern, then the residual series should show no autocorrelation
at the season's lag. Figure 6.12 displays the autocorrelations
for the residuals from the regression model with seasonality
and quadratic trend shown in Figure 6.8. It is clear that the 6-
month (and 12-month) cyclical behavior no longer dominates the
series of residuals, indicating that the regression model captured
them adequately. However, we can also see a strong positive
autocorrelation from lag-1 on, indicating a positive relationship
between neighboring residuals. This is valuable information,
which can be used to improve forecasting.

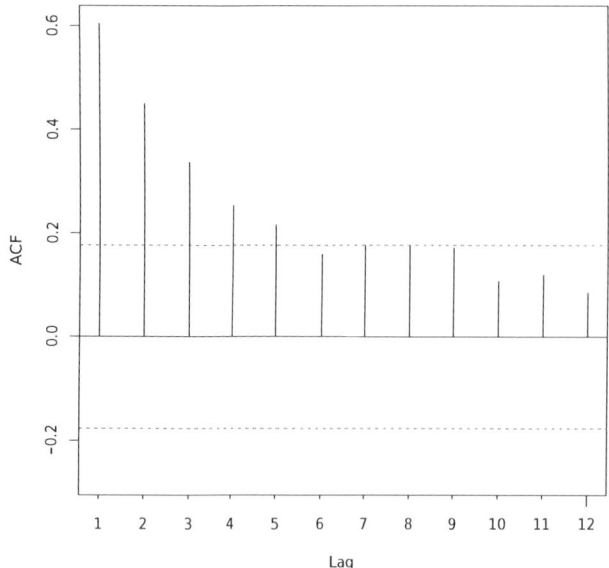

Figure 6.12: Acf output of autocorrelations of residual series from Figure 6.8.

Improving Forecasts by Integrating Autocorrelation Information

In general, there are two approaches to taking advantage of autocorrelation. One is by directly building the autocorrelation into the regression model, and the other is by constructing a second-level forecasting model on the residual series.

Among regression-type models that directly account for autocorrelation are autoregressive (AR) models, or the more general class of models called ARIMA models (AutoRegressive Integrated Moving-Average). Autoregressive models are similar to linear regression models, except that the predictors are the past values of the series. For example, an autoregression model of order 2 (AR(2)), can be written as

$$y_t = \beta_0 + \beta_1 y_{t-1} + \beta_2 y_{t-2} + \epsilon_t \qquad (6.5)$$

Estimating such models is roughly equivalent to fitting a linear regression model with the series as the output, and the lagged series (at lag-1 and 2 in this example) as the predictors. However, it is better to use designated ARIMA estimation methods (e.g., those available in the `forecast` package's `Arima` function) over ordinary linear regression estimation, to produce more accurate results.[6] Moving from AR to ARIMA models creates a larger set of more flexible forecasting models but also requires much more statistical expertise. Even with the simpler AR models, fitting them to raw time series that contain patterns such as trends and seasonality requires the user to perform several initial data transformations and to choose the order of the model. These are not straightforward tasks. Because ARIMA modeling is less robust and requires more experience and statistical expertise than other methods, the use of such models for forecasting raw series is generally less popular in practical forecasting. We therefore direct the interested reader to classic time series textbooks.[7]

Here we discuss one particular use of AR models that is straightforward to apply in the context of forecasting, and which can provide significant improvement to short-term forecasts. This relates to the second approach for utilizing autocorrelation, which requires constructing a second-level forecasting model for the residuals, as follows:

1. Generate k-step-ahead forecast of the series (F_{t+k}), using a forecasting method.

2. Generate k-step-ahead forecast of forecast error (e_{t+k}), using an AR (or other) model.

3. Improve the initial k-step-ahead forecast of the series by adjusting it according to its forecasted error: Improved $F^*_{t+k} = F_{t+k} + e_{t+k}$.

In particular, we can fit low-order AR models to series of residuals (or forecast errors) that can then be used to forecast future forecast errors. By fitting the series of residuals, rather than the raw series, we avoid the need for initial data transformations (because the residual series is not expected to contain any trends or cyclical behavior besides autocorrelation).

To fit an AR model to the series of residuals, we first examine the autocorrelations of the residual series. We then choose the order of the AR model according to the lags in which autocorre-

[6] ARIMA model estimation differs from ordinary regression estimation by accounting for the dependence between observations.

[7] For example, Chapter 4 in
C. Chatfield. *The Analysis of Time Series: An Introduction*. Chapman & Hall/CRC, 6th edition, 2003

lation appears. Often, when autocorrelation exists at lag-1 and higher, it is sufficient to fit an AR(1) model of the form

$$e_t = \beta_0 + \beta_1 e_{t-1} + \epsilon_t \tag{6.6}$$

where e_t denotes the residual (or forecast error) at time t. For example, although the autocorrelations in Figure 6.12 appear large from lags 1 to 10 or so, it is likely that an AR(1) would capture all these relationships. The reason is that if neighboring values are correlated, then the relationship can propagate to values that are two periods away, then three periods away, and so forth.

An AR(1) model fitted to the Amtrak ridership residual series is shown in Figure 6.13. The corresponding R code and model output are also shown in Figure 6.13.[8] The AR(1) coefficient (0.5998) is close to the lag-1 autocorrelation (0.6041) that we found earlier (Figure 6.12).

The forecasted residual for April 2001 is computed by plugging in the most recent residual from March 2001 (equal to 12.108) into the AR(1) model: 0.3728 + (0.5998)(12.108) = 7.635. The positive value tells us that the regression model will produce a ridership forecast for April 2001 that is too low and that we should adjust it up by adding 7,635 riders. In this particular example, the regression model (with quadratic trend and seasonality) produced a forecast of 2,004,271 riders, and the improved two-stage model [regression + AR(1) correction] corrected it by increasing it to 2,011,906 riders. The actual value for April 2003 turned out to be 2,023,792 riders – much closer to the improved forecast.

Finally, from the plot of the actual versus fitted residual series, we can see that the AR(1) model fits the residual series quite well. Note, however, that the plot is based on the training period (until March 2001). To evaluate predictive performance of the two-level model [regression + AR(1)], we would have to examine performance (e.g., via MAPE or RMSE metrics) on the validation period, in a fashion similar to the calculation that we performed for April 2001 above.

To fit an AR model, we use an ARIMA model of order $(p, 0, 0)$. The order (p, d, q) of an ARIMA process refers to its three main

[8] The function Arima in the forecast package fits and forecasts ARIMA models (which includes as a subset AR models). The order (1,0,0) refers to an AR(1) process.

code for creating Figure 6.13 and output of AR(1) model

```
train.lm.trend.season <- tslm(train.ts ~ trend + I(trend^2) + season)
train.res.arima <- Arima(train.lm.trend.season$residuals, order = c(1,0,0))

plot(train.lm.trend.season$residuals, ylim = c(-250, 250),  ylab = "Residuals",
    xlab = "Time", bty = "l", xaxt = "n", xlim = c(1991,2006.25), main = "")
axis(1, at = seq(1991, 2006, 1), labels = format(seq(1991, 2006, 1)))
lines(train.res.arima.pred$fitted, lwd = 2, col = "blue")

> summary(train.res.arima)
Series: train.lm.trend.season$residuals
ARIMA(1,0,0) with non-zero mean

Coefficients:
         ar1  intercept
      0.5998     0.3728
s.e.  0.0712    11.8408

sigma^2 estimated as 2829:  log likelihood=-663.54
AIC=1333.08    AICc=1333.29    BIC=1341.52
```

Figure 6.13: Fitting an AR(1) model to the residual series from Figure 6.8.

features. p is the number of autoregressive (AR) terms in the model, q is the number of moving average (MA) terms, and d is the number of integrated terms (or number of times the series is differenced before an ARMA model is applied). To learn more about how to fit ARIMA models in R and use them in forecasting, see Chapter 8 of the online textbook *Forecasting: Principles and Practice* by Hyndman and Athanasopoulos at www.otexts.org/fpp/8.

Finally, to examine whether we have indeed accounted for the autocorrelation in the series, and that no more information remains in the series, we examine the autocorrelations of the series of residuals-of-residuals [the residuals obtained after the AR(1), which was applied to the regression residuals]. This can be seen in Figure 6.14. It is clear that no more autocorrelation remains, and that the addition of the AR(1) model has captured the autocorrelation information adequately.

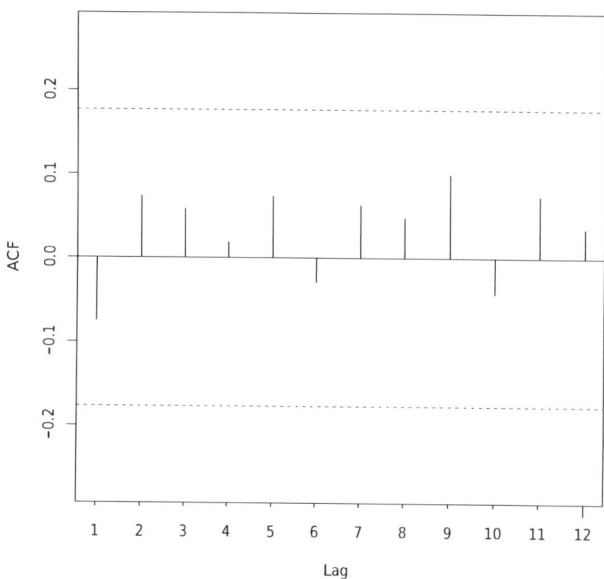

Figure 6.14: Autocorrelations of residuals-of-residuals series

We mentioned earlier that improving forecasts via an additional AR layer is useful for short-term forecasting. The reason is that an AR model of order k will usually only provide useful forecasts for the next k periods, and after that forecasts will rely on earlier forecasts rather than on actual data. For example, to forecast the residual of May 2001, when the time of prediction is March 2001, we would need the residual for April 2001. However, because that value is not available, it would be replaced by its forecast. Hence, the forecast for May 2001 would be based on the forecast for April 2001.

Evaluating Predictability

Before attempting to forecast a time series, it is important to determine whether it is predictable, in the sense that its past (non-trivially) predicts its future. One useful way to assess predictability is to test whether the series is a random walk. A *random walk* is a series in which changes from one time period to the next are random. According to the efficient market hypothesis in economics, asset prices are random walks and therefore predicting stock prices is a game of chance.[9]

A random walk is a special case of an AR(1) model, where the slope coefficient is equal to 1:

$$y_t = \beta_0 + y_{t-1} + \epsilon_t. \tag{6.7}$$

We see from this equation that the difference between the values at periods $t-1$ and t is random, hence the term random walk. Forecasts from such a model are basically equal to the most recent observed value, reflecting the lack of any other information. Furthermore, with a symmetric distribution for the errors, the forecast that a random walk will go up is always a coin flip (50%). Consequently, economists refer to such time series as "unpredictable". Technically though, you can make a forecast about a random walk. The trouble, however, is that the forecast is naive, and anyone can do it.

To test whether a series is a random walk, we fit an AR(1) model and test the hypothesis that the slope coefficient is equal to 1 ($H_0 : \beta_1 = 1$ vs. $H_1 : \beta_1 \neq 1$). If the hypothesis is rejected

[9] There is some controversy surrounding the efficient market hypothesis, claiming that the slight autocorrelation in asset prices does make them predictable to some extent. However, transaction costs and bid-ask spreads tend to offset any prediction benefits.

(reflected by a small p-value), then the series is not a random walk, and we can attempt to predict it (with something beyond the naive forecast).

As an example, consider the AR(1) model fitted to the residuals as shown in Figure 6.13. The slope coefficient (0.5998) is more than 5 standard errors away from 1, indicating that this is not a random walk. In contrast, consider the AR(1) model fitted to the series of S&P500 monthly closing prices between May 1995 and August 2003 (available in *SP500.xls*.) The slope coefficient is 0.9833, with a standard error of 0.0145. The coefficient is sufficiently close to 1 (around one standard error away), indicating that this may not be a random walk.[10] Forecasting this series using any of the methods described earlier is therefore not likely to improve over the naive forecast.

Another approach for evaluating predictability, which is mathematically equivalent to the above approach, is to examine the series of differences between each pair of consecutive values $(y_t - y_{t-1})$. This is called the *lag-1 differenced series* (see also Section 5.3 in Chapter 5). For example, we can obtain the differenced series for the ridership data by subtracting column C from column B in Figure 6.10. Examine Equation (6.7), and subtract y_{t-1} from both sides. We see that a random walk is equal to a constant plus a random term. Hence, to test whether a series is a random walk, we compute the differenced series and then examine the ACF plot of the differenced series. If the ACF plot indicates that the autocorrelations at lags 1,2,3, etc. are all approximately zero (all the bars are within the thresholds), then we can infer that the original series is a random walk.

6.5 Irregular Patterns

In this chapter we described how linear regression models can be useful forecasters by capturing trend and seasonality patterns of various types as well as autocorrelation (via autoregressive models). Regression models can also capture or handle additional types of patterns that are common in real time series data: outliers, special events, and missing values. Let us consider each separately.

[10] A more advanced way to test whether a time series is non-stationary (e.g., a random walk) is to use the Augmented Dickey-Fuller test. In R, the function adf.test in the tseries package applies this test. In the case of the S&P500 monthly closing prices, the test suggests the series is non-stationary and may be a random walk.

Outliers

Outliers are extreme data values. As in cross-sectional linear regression, a fitted regression model can be greatly affected (distorted) by outliers. Hence, if the training period contains one or more outliers, it is important to carefully assess their effect on the estimated model. To do this, we fit the model with and without the outliers and see how much the predictive performance is affected. If dropping the outlier(s) does not have much effect, then we can fit the model with the outlier(s).

An alternative to removing outliers from the training set is to "label" them as outliers and incorporate them into the model. This is done by using a dummy variable which takes the value 1 for periods with outliers and zero otherwise, and incorporating it as an additional predictor in the regression model.

Special Events

In some cases, the values in a series are expected to be extreme due to an expected event. Unlike regular patterns such as weekend/weekdays, special events have a known schedule but are less regular than seasonal patterns and are typically shorter. One example of special events is holidays, which affect series such as customer arrivals and sales. Holidays can pose a challenge especially when considering more than a single calendar.[11] Another example is sporting events or music concerts, which affect traffic, accident rates, and more.

Special events can be incorporated into a regression model by using a dummy variable in the model building stage, in the performance evaluation stage, and in the forecasting step. The dummy variable obtains the value 1 for periods with special events and zero otherwise.

During the model building stage, the dummy variable captures special events that took place during the training period and is incorporated as a predictor into the regression model. The same predictor is used to capture special events in the validation period for evaluating predictive power. And finally, the dummy variable is used for forecasting future periods that might include special events.

Figure 6.15: Sporting events affect many time series. (Image by kanate / FreeDigitalPhotos.net)

[11] For example, lunar calendar holidays (such as Jewish, Muslim, Hindu and Buddhist holidays) fall on different dates of the Gregorian calendar each year.

6.6   Problems

1. *Impact of September 11 on Air Travel in the United States:* The Research and Innovative Technology Administration's Bureau of Transportation Statistics (BTS) conducted a study to evaluate the impact of the September 11, 2001, terrorist attack on U.S. transportation. The study report and the data can be found at `www.bts.gov/publications/estimated_impacts_of_9_11_on_us_travel`. The goal of the study was stated as follows:

Figure 6.16: Air travel. (Image by africa / FreeDigitalPhotos.net)

> The purpose of this study is to provide a greater understanding of the passenger travel behavior patterns of persons making long distance trips before and after September 11.

The report analyzes monthly passenger movement data between January 1990 and April 2004. Data on three monthly time series are given in the file *Sept11Travel.xls* for this period: (1) actual airline revenue passenger miles (Air), (2) rail passenger miles (Rail), and (3) vehicle miles traveled (Auto).

In order to assess the impact of September 11, BTS took the following approach: Using data before September 11, it forecasted future data (under the assumption of no terrorist attack). Then, BTS compared the forecasted series with the actual data to assess the impact of the event. Our first step, therefore, is to split each of the time series into two parts: pre- and post-September 11. We now concentrate only on the earlier time series.

(a) Plot the pre-event Air time series. Which time series components appear from the plot?

(b) The figure below is a time plot of the *seasonally adjusted* pre-September-11 Air series. Which of the following methods would be adequate for forecasting this series?

  • Linear regression model with dummy variables
  • Linear regression model with trend
  • Linear regression model with dummy variables and trend

(c) Specify a linear regression model for the Air series that would produce a seasonally adjusted series similar to the

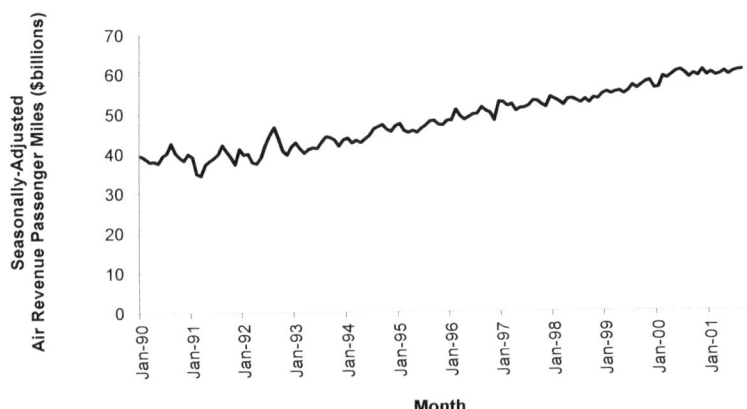

Figure 6.17: Seasonally
adjusted pre-September-11
air series

one shown in (b), with multiplicative seasonality. What is
the output variable? What are the predictors?

(d) Run the regression model from (c). Remember to create
dummy variables for the months and to use only pre-event
data.

  i. What can we learn from the statistical insignificance of
  the coefficients for October and September?

  ii. The actual value of Air (air revenue passenger miles) in
  January 1990 was 35.153577 billion. What is the residual
  for this month, using the regression model? Report the
  residual in terms of air revenue passenger miles.

(e) Create an ACF (autocorrelation) plot of the regression
residuals.

  i. What does the ACF plot tell us about the regression
  model's forecasts?

  ii. How can this information be used to improve the
  model?

(f) Fit linear regression models to Air, Rail and Auto with
additive seasonality and an appropriate trend. For Air and
Auto, fit a linear trend. For Rail, use a quadratic trend.
Remember to use only pre-event data. Once the models are
estimated, use them to forecast each of the three post-event
series.

i. For each series (Air, Rail, Auto), plot the complete pre-event and post-event actual series overlaid with the predicted series.

ii. What can be said about the effect of the September 11 terrorist attack on the three modes of transportation? Discuss the magnitude of the effect, its time span, and any other relevant aspect.

2. *Analysis of Canadian Manufacturing Workers Work-Hours:* The time series plot below describes the average annual number of weekly hours spent by Canadian manufacturing workers (data available in *CanadianWorkHours.xls*, courtesy of Ken Black).

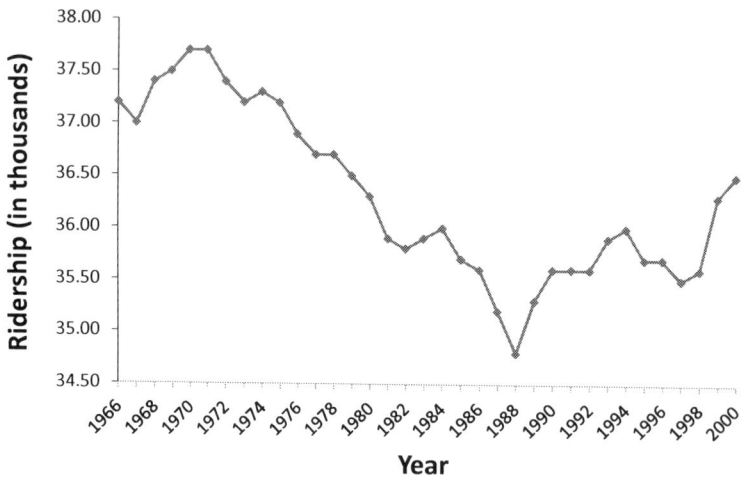

Figure 6.18: Average annual weekly hours spent by Canadian manufacturing workers

(a) Which one model of the following regression-based models would fit the series best?

- Linear trend model
- Linear trend model with seasonality
- Quadratic trend model
- Quadratic trend model with seasonality

(b) If we computed the autocorrelation of this series, would the lag-1 autocorrelation exhibit negative, positive, or no autocorrelation? How can you see this from the plot?

(c) Compute the autocorrelation and produce an ACF plot. Verify your answer to the previous question.

3. *Regression Modeling of Toys "R" Us Revenues:* The figure below is a time series plot of the quarterly revenues of Toys "R" Us between 1992 and 1995 (thanks to Chris Albright for suggesting the use of these data, available in *ToysRUsRevenues.xls*).

Figure 6.19: Toys. (Image by digitalart / FreeDigitalPhotos.net)

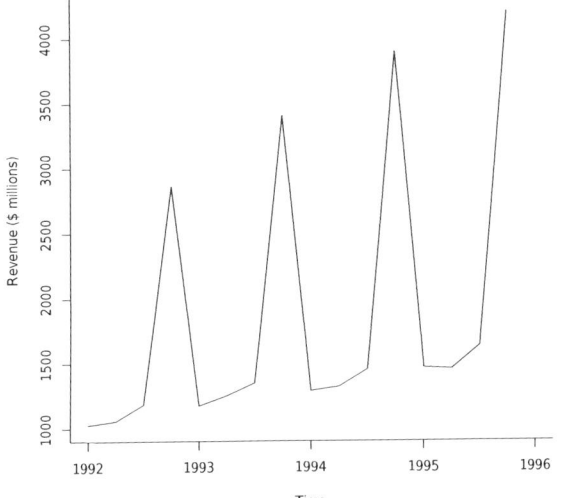

Figure 6.20: Quarterly revenues of Toys "R" Us, 1992-1995.

(a) Fit a regression model with a linear trend and seasonal dummy variables. Use the entire series (excluding the last two quarters) as the training period.

(b) A partial output of the regression model is shown in Table 6.6 (where season2 is the Quarter 2 dummy). Use this output to answer the following questions:

i. Mention two statistics (and their values) that measure how well this model fits the training period.

ii. Mention two statistics (and their values) that measure the predictive accuracy of this model.

iii. After adjusting for trend, what is the average difference between sales in Q3 and sales in Q1?

iv. After adjusting for seasonality, which quarter (Q1, Q2, Q3 or Q4) has the highest average sales?

Table 6.6: Regression model fitted to Toys "R" Us time series and its predictive performance in training and validation periods.

```
Coefficients:
              Estimate Std. Error t value Pr(>|t|)
(Intercept)   906.75      115.35    7.861 2.55e-05 ***
trend          47.11       11.26    4.185  0.00236 **
season2       -15.11      119.66   -0.126  0.90231
season3        89.17      128.67    0.693  0.50582
season4      2101.73      129.17   16.272 5.55e-08 ***
---
Signif. codes:  0 *** 0.001 ** 0.01 * 0.05 .

                   ME     RMSE      MAE       MPE      MAPE      MASE
Training set   0.0000 135.0795 92.53061 0.1614994 5.006914 0.4342122
Test set     183.1429 313.6820 254.66667 3.0193814 7.404655 1.1950571
```

4. *Forecasting Wal-Mart Stock:* Figure 6.21 shows a time plot of Wal-Mart daily closing prices between February 2001 and February 2002. (Thanks to Chris Albright for suggesting the use of these data, publicly available at finance.yahoo.com and in *WalMartStock.xls*.). The ACF plots of these daily closing prices and its lag-1 differenced series are in Figure 6.22. Table 6.7 shows the output from fitting an AR(1) model to the series of closing prices and to the series of differences. Use all the information to answer the following questions.

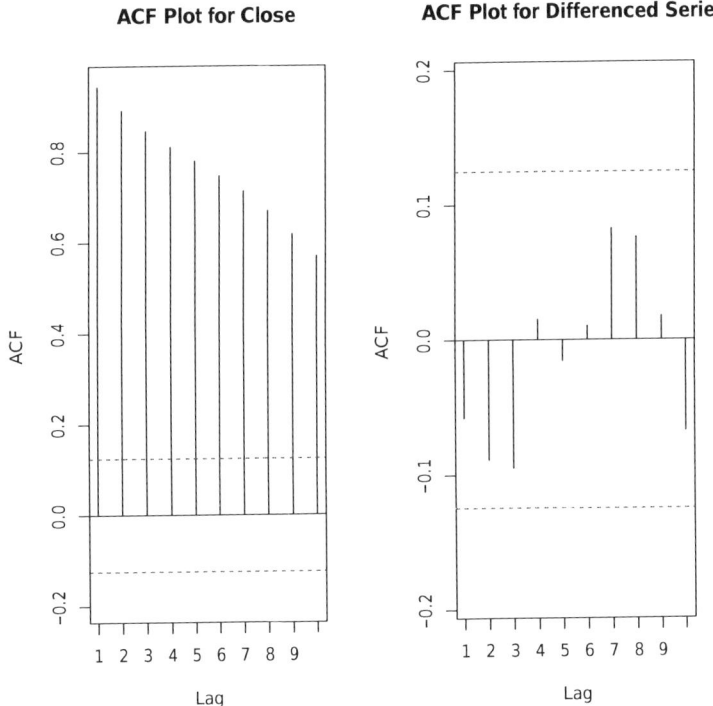

Figure 6.21: Daily closing price of Wal-Mart stock, February 2001-2002

Figure 6.22: ACF plots for the Wal-Mart stock series and its lag-1 differenced series.

Table 6.7: Output of fitting AR(1) models to the Wal-Mart stock series and the differenced series.

```
Series: close.ts                    Series: diff(close.ts, 1)
ARIMA(1,0,0) with non-zero mean     ARIMA(1,0,0) with non-zero mean

Coefficients:                       Coefficients:
         ar1  intercept                      ar1  intercept
      0.9558    52.9497                   -0.0579    0.0207
s.e.  0.0187     1.3280             s.e.   0.0635    0.0599
```

(a) Create a time plot of the differenced series.

(b) Which of the following is/are relevant for testing whether this stock is a random walk?

- The autocorrelations of the closing price series
- The AR(1) slope coefficient for the closing price series
- The AR(1) constant coefficient for the closing price series
- The autocorrelations of the differenced series
- The AR(1) slope coefficient for the differenced series
- The AR(1) constant coefficient for the differenced series

(c) Recreate the AR(1) model output for the Close price series shown in the left of Table 6.7. Does the AR model indicate that this is a random walk? Explain how you reached your conclusion.

(d) What are the implications of finding that a time series is a random walk? Choose the correct statement(s) below.

- It is impossible to obtain useful forecasts of the series.
- The series is random.
- The changes in the series from one period to the other are random.

5. *Forecasting Department Store Sales:* The time series plot shown in Figure 6.24 describes actual quarterly sales for a department store over a 6-year period. (Data available in *DepartmentStoreSales.xls*, courtesy of Chris Albright.)

(a) The forecaster decided that there is an exponential trend in the series. In order to fit a regression-based model that accounts for this trend, which of the following operations must be performed (either manually or by a function in R)?

Figure 6.23: (Image by Paul Martin Eldridge / FreeDigitalPhotos.net)

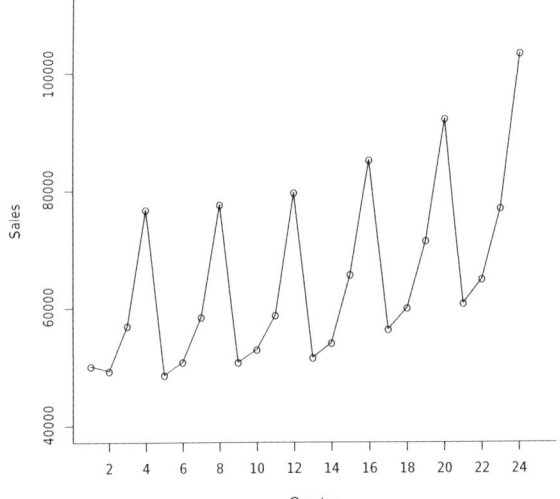

Figure 6.24: Department
store quarterly sales series.

- Take a logarithm of the Quarter index
- Take a logarithm of sales
- Take an exponent of sales
- Take an exponent of Quarter index

(b) Fit a regression model with an exponential trend and
seasonality, using only the first 20 quarters as the training
period (remember to first partition the series into training
and validation periods).

(c) A partial output is shown in Table 6.8. From the output,
after adjusting for trend, are Q2 average sales higher, lower,
or approximately equal to the average Q1 sales?

(d) Use this model to forecast sales in quarters 21 and 22.

(e) The plots shown in Figure 6.25 describe the fit (top) and
forecast errors (bottom) from this regression model.

   i. Recreate these plots.

   ii. Based on these plots, what can you say about your forecasts for quarters Q21 and Q22? Are they likely to over-
forecast, under-forecast, or be reasonably close to the real
sales values?

```
> summary(tslm(sales.ts ~ trend + season, lambda = 0))

Coefficients:
             Estimate Std. Error t value Pr(>|t|)
(Intercept) 10.748945   0.018725 574.057  < 2e-16 ***
trend        0.011088   0.001295   8.561 3.70e-07 ***
season2      0.024956   0.020764   1.202    0.248
season3      0.165343   0.020884   7.917 9.79e-07 ***
season4      0.433746   0.021084  20.572 2.10e-12 ***
---
Signif. codes:  0 *** 0.001 ** 0.01 * 0.05 .
```

Table 6.8: Output from regression model fit to department store sales in the training period.

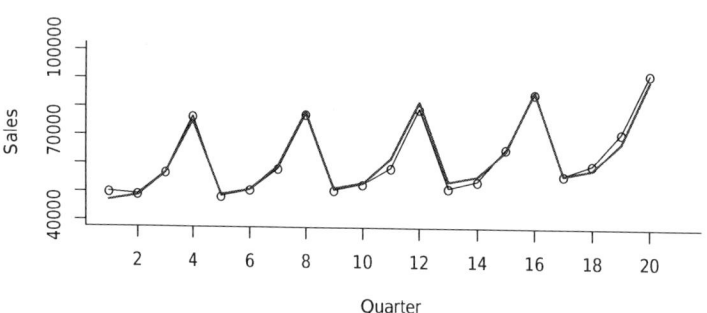

Figure 6.25: Fit of regression model for department store sales.

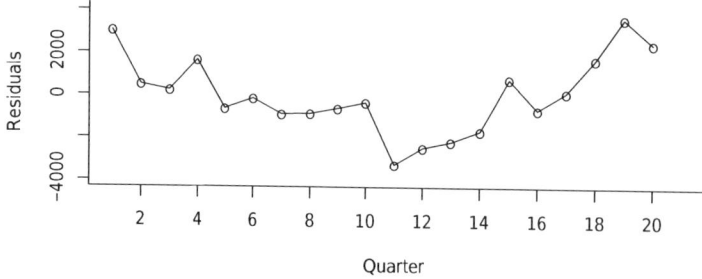

(f) Looking at the residual plot, which of the following statements appear true?

- Seasonality is not captured well.
- The regression model fits the data well.

(g) The trend in the data is not captured well by the model.
Which of the following solutions is adequate and a parsimonious solution for improving model fit?

- Fit a quadratic trend model to the residuals (with *Quarter*
  and *Quarter*^{2}.)
- Fit an AR model to the residuals.
- Fit a quadratic trend model to Sales (with *Quarter* and
  Quarter^2.)

6. *Souvenir Sales:* The file *SouvenirSales.xls* contains monthly sales
for a souvenir shop at a beach resort town in Queensland,
Australia, between 1995 and 2001. [source: Hyndman, R. J.
Time Series Data Library, `http://data.is/TSDLdemo`; accessed
on July 13, 2015.]

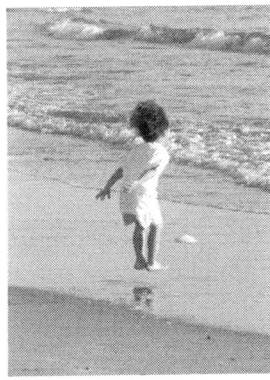

Figure 6.26: Beach Resort.
(Image by quyenlan /
FreeDigitalPhotos.net)

Back in 2001, the store wanted to use the data to forecast sales
for the next 12 months (year 2002). They hired an analyst
to generate forecasts. The analyst first partitioned the data
into training and validation periods, with the validation set
containing the last 12 months of data (year 2001). She then fit
a regression model to sales, using the training period.

(a) Based on the two time plots in Figure 6.27, which predictors should be included in the regression model? What is
the total number of predictors in the model?

(b) Run a regression model with Sales (in Australian dollars)
as the output variable and with a linear trend and monthly
predictors. Remember to fit only the training period. Call
this model A.

i. Examine the estimated coefficients: Which month tends
to have the highest average sales during the year? Why
is this reasonable?

ii. What does the estimated trend coefficient of model A
mean?

Figure 6.27: Monthly sales at Australian souvenir shop in dollars (top) and in log scale (bottom)

(c) Run a regression model with log(Sales) as the output variable and with a linear trend and monthly predictors. Remember to fit only the training period. Call this model B.

  i. Fitting a model to log(Sales) with a linear trend is equivalent to fitting a model to Sales (in dollars) with what type of trend?

  ii. What does the estimated trend coefficient of model B mean?

  iii. Use this model to forecast the sales in February 2002.

(d) Compare the two regression models (A and B) in terms of forecast performance. Which model is preferable for forecasting? Mention at least two reasons based on the information in the outputs.

(e) Continuing with model B, create an ACF plot until lag-15 for the forecast errors. Now fit an AR model with lag-2 [ARIMA(2, 0, 0)] to the forecast errors.

  i. Examining the ACF plot and the estimated coefficients of the AR(2) model (and their statistical significance), what can we learn about the forecasts that result from model B?

  ii. Use the autocorrelation information to compute a forecast for January 2002, using model B and the AR(2) model above.

(f) How would you model these data differently if the goal is understanding the different components of sales in the souvenir shop between 1995 and 2001? Mention two differences.

7. *Shipments of Household Appliances:* The file *ApplianceShipments.xls* contains the series of quarterly shipments (in millions of USD) of U.S. household appliances between 1985 and 1989 (data courtesy of Ken Black). The series is plotted in Figure 6.29.

(a) If we compute the autocorrelation of the series, which lag (> 0) is most likely to have the largest coefficient (in absolute value)?

Figure 6.28: (Image by Salvatore Vuono / FreeDigitalPhotos.net)

(b) Create an ACF plot and compare it with your answer.

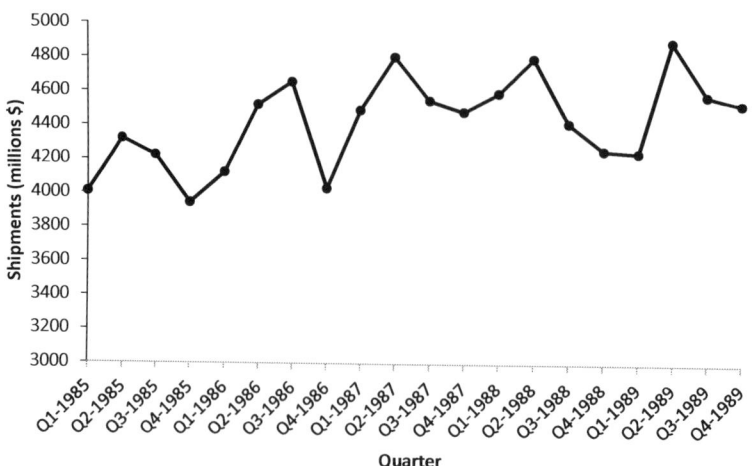

Figure 6.29: Quarterly shipments of U.S. household appliances over 5 years

8. *Forecasting Australian Wine Sales:* Figure 6.31 shows time plots of monthly sales of six types of Australian wines (red, rose, sweet white, dry white, sparkling, and fortified) for 1980-1994. [Data available in *AustralianWines.xls* [source: Hyndman, R. J. Time Series Data Library, http://data.is/TSDLdemo; accessed on July 13, 2015.] The units are thousands of liters. You are hired to obtain short-term forecasts (2-3 months ahead) for each of the six series, and this task will be repeated every month.

(a) Which forecasting method would you choose if you had to choose the same method for all series? Why?

(b) Fortified wine has the largest market share of the six types of wine considered. You are asked to focus on fortified wine sales alone and produce as accurate as possible forecast for the next 2 months.

Figure 6.30: (Image by Naypong / FreeDigitalPhotos.net)

   • Start by partitioning the data using the period until December 1993 as the training period.

   • Fit a regression model to sales with a linear trend and seasonality.

    i. Create the "actual vs. forecast" plot. What can you say about model fit?

    ii. Use the regression model to forecast sales in January and February 1994.

(c) Create an ACF plot for the residuals from the above model until lag-12.

    i. Examining this plot, which of the following statements are reasonable?

- Decembers (month 12) are not captured well by the model.

- There is a strong correlation between sales on the same calendar month.

- The model does not capture the seasonality well.

- We should try to fit an autoregressive model with lag-12 to the residuals.

    ii. How can you handle the above effect without adding another layer to your model?

Sweet Wine Sales

Rose Wine Sales

Sparkling Wine Sales

Red Wine Sales

Dry White Wine Sales

Fortified Wine Sales

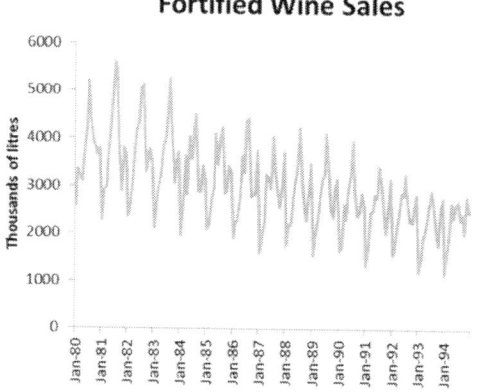

Figure 6.31: Monthly sales of six types of Australian wines between 1980 - 1994

7
Other Forecasting Methods

The methods covered in Chapters 5 and 6 are the most popular in business forecasting. In this chapter, we present two additional methods: logistic regression and neural networks. Both methods are commonly used for prediction with cross-sectional data, but they can also be used in a time series context. We introduce these methods in order to expand the discussion of forecasting to *binary forecasts* (event/no-event), and to the inclusion of *external information*.

Section 7.1 discusses the inclusion of external predictor information, and general principals guiding such inclusion. Section 7.2 describes the context of binary forecasting, where the goal is to forecast whether an event or non-event will occur in future periods. We discuss naive forecasts and performance evaluation in the context of binary outcome forecasting. Sections 7.3 and 7.4 introduce the two methods of logistic regression and neural networks. Logistic regression is a model-based method that can be used for forecasting binary outcomes. Neural networks are very flexible data-driven algorithms suitable for forecasting numerical and binary data. Both methods can be used for extrapolation as well as for inclusion of external information.

7.1 *Including External Information*

Chapter 4 described the difference between econometric models, where the inclusion of external information is based on a causal theoretical model, and forecasting methods that include external information that improves the accuracy of predictions, regardless of whether a causal model is present. In other words, we include information that is *correlated* with the series of interest, and which shows improved forecast accuracy. While there might be many external series that are correlated with the series of interest, there are two limitations on what external information to include and how such information is included in the model. One affects the values of the predictors and the other affects the estimated forecasting model itself. We describe each of these considerations next.

Consideration #1: Lagged or Forecasted Predictors

Recall that all predictor information must be available at the time of prediction. If the time of prediction is t, then the forecasting model should include either lagged versions of the external information ($x_{t-1}, x_{t-2}, \ldots$) or forecasts of external information that is unavailable at the time of prediction. Availability of information refers not only to past vs. future, but also to lag times in acquiring the external data.

Consider the example from Chapter 4 of using information on weekly gas prices for forecasting weekly airfare. While the two series (gas prices and airfare) might be highly correlated, airfare forecasts can only use *already known* gas prices or *forecasted* gas prices. In other words, we can build models of the form

$$\text{(airfare)}_t = \beta_0 + \beta_1 \text{(gas price)}_{t-1} + \epsilon \qquad (7.1)$$

and use the already-known gas price from last week, if such data are available in a timely manner. Or, we can build the model

$$\text{(airfare)}_t = \beta_0 + \beta_1 \text{(forecasted gas price)}_t + \epsilon \qquad (7.2)$$

which includes an unknown gas price value, and hence requires building a separate model for forecasting weekly gas prices (in itself a harder task, and if the forecast is accurate, a more lucrative one).

Consideration #2: Training Period and Model Updating

With time series forecasting, it is advantageous to update the model as new information arrives. With regression-type models, updating leads to new β coefficients. Continuous updating requires assuring that the model is trained only on data that are available at the time of prediction. The training period must therefore take into account data availability and the forecast horizon.

For example, for forecasting one-week-ahead airfare rates, the forecasting model must be trained only on data that are available up to the time of prediction. This depends on how quickly we receive prior weekly airfare and gas price figures. Any lag time in acquiring the information must be taken into account in choosing the training period. A lag time of two weeks requires shifting the training period two weeks back, thereby requiring 3-step-ahead forecasts. In other words, even when training data are available right up to the time of prediction, if in practice we will have a two week lag in getting data, we must not include the last two weeks of training data in the model (though we *can* include forecasts of those data from a separate model).

Careful attention to the choice of training period is needed not only for producing forecasts but also when evaluating predictive performance. Validation period forecasts should be based on models that were estimated/trained only on data that were available at the "time of prediction".

Example: Forecasting Crop Yield

Regression models with external information predictors are common in agriculture for forecasting crop yield. We use one such example to elucidate the issues of predictor choice and training period. Tannura et al. (2008) [1] developed linear regression models for forecasting annual soybean and corn yield in the United States "Corn Belt" (Iowa, Illinois and Indiana) based on data from 1960-2006. Their forecasting model includes a linear trend to capture technological advances in agriculture as well as external weather predictors: average monthly precipitation ($x_1 = prec$)

[1] M. A. Tannura, S. H. Irwin, and D. L. Good. Weather, technology, and corn and soybean yields in the U.S. corn belt. Marketing and Outlook Research Report 2008-01, Department of Agricultural and Consumer Economics, University of Illinois at Urbana-Champaign, 2008

and average monthly temperature ($x_2 = temp$).[2] The model for yield in year t is:

[2] The quadratic precipitation terms represent the effect of heavy summer rainfall on yield.

$$
\begin{aligned}
(\text{yield})_t \; = \; & \beta_0 + \beta_1 t + \beta_2 (\text{Sept through April prec})_t \\
& + \; \beta_3 (\text{May prec})_t + \beta_4 (\text{June prec})_t + \beta_5 (\text{June prec})_t^2 \\
& + \; \beta_6 (\text{July prec})_t + \beta_7 (\text{July prec})_t^2 + \beta_8 (\text{Aug prec})_t + \beta_9 (\text{Aug prec})_t^2 \\
& + \; \beta_{10} (\text{May temp})_t + \beta_{11} (\text{June temp})_t + \beta_{12} (\text{July temp})_t + \beta_{13} (\text{Aug temp})_t + \epsilon
\end{aligned}
$$

This model is intended to produce annual forecasts on the first day of June, July, August, September and October each year (assuming that later forecasts will be more accurate due to increased weather information). To assure that the model is based only on information available at the time of prediction, two steps were taken by the researchers:

1. To produce forecasts in a certain year, the regression model is estimated using data only up to the prior year. For example, to produce forecasts for 2005, the regression model is estimated using weather data only until Dec 2004. This approach was also used for performance evaluation: forecasts for each year in the validation period were based on estimating the model on weather data only up to the prior year.

2. On a day when a forecast is generated, actual temperature and precipitation values for that year are entered only for months prior to that date (and hence the subscript t). For later months, the average monthly temperature and precipitation in previous years is used.

Example: Forecasting Box-office Revenue

In the article "Predicting the Future With Social Media"[3], the authors build a linear regression model for forecasting box-office revenue generated by a movie in its opening weekend. Their predictors are based on "tweets", which are posts placed on the online social networking and microblogging service www.twitter.com, that referred to movies prior to their release. The daily tweet rate (TR) from each of the last seven days was included as seven predictors, as well as the number of theaters in

[3] S. Asur and B. A. Huberman. Predicting the future with social media. In *IEEE/WIC/ACM International Conference on Web Intelligence and Intelligent Agent Technology (WI-IAT)*, pages 492 – 499, 2010

which the movie was to be released. Their model for box-office revenues for a movie on the opening week (day t) is given by:

$$
\begin{aligned}
\text{(Box-office revenue)}_t \;=\; & \beta_0 + \beta_1 \text{TR}_{t-1} + \beta_2 \text{TR}_{t-2} + \beta_3 \text{TR}_{t-3} + \beta_4 \text{TR}_{t-4} \\
+\; & \beta_5 \text{TR}_{t-5} + \beta_6 \text{TR}_{t-6} + \beta_7 \text{TR}_{t-7} + \beta_8 (\# \text{ Theaters})_t + \epsilon
\end{aligned}
$$

The authors stress two issues related to predictor availability:

1. "In all cases, we are using only data available prior to the release to predict box-office for the opening weekend." This includes the number of theaters, which is known in advance.

2. "Note however, that since historical information on tweets are not available [retroactively], we were able to use data only [for] the movies we have collected"

The latter point relates to practical use of the forecasting model, where the needed predictor information requires special data collection.

7.2   Forecasting Binary Outcomes

While classic time series forecasting deals with numerical data, there is often a need to forecast series of binary events. One example is forecasting the direction of stock price movements (up/down). A second example is forecasting whether a health, environmental or other indicator will cross a certain threshold (e.g., blood sugar level, air pollution level, or credit card spending). A third example is forecasting the occurrence of an event such as a recession or testing positive for a disease. In such scenarios, it is likely that the outcome is related to outcomes in previous periods. Hence, as in numerical forecasting, we aim to capture systematic components such as trend, seasonality and autocorrelation. In this section, we describe a popular forecasting method for binary outcomes called *logistic regression*. In Section 7.4 the forecasting method of neural networks is introduced, which is also suitable for forecasting binary outcomes.

Naive Forecasts and Performance Evaluation

As in numerical forecasting, a naive forecast can simply be the binary value in the previous period. An alternative naive benchmark is the "majority-class" forecast, that is, the most popular outcome in the training period: event or non-event. When more than 50% of the training period outcomes are "events", then a naive majority-class forecast is "event". When fewer than 50% of the training period outcomes are "events", then the majority-class forecast is "non-event".

The performance of a binary outcome forecasting method is evaluated by comparing the binary forecasts to the actual binary events. This comparison is commonly presented in a 2 × 2 table, called a *classification matrix*. The table shows the correct and erroneous forecasts of events and of non-events, as illustrated in Table 7.1. As in numerical forecasting, we evaluate performance using the validation period.

	predicted events	**predicted non-events**
actual events	# correctly forecasted events	# missed events
actual non-events	# missed non-events	# correctly forecasted non-events

Table 7.1: Classification matrix for evaluating predictive performance of binary outcome forecasts (computed on the validation period)

There are various performance measures that are computed from the classification matrix values. In addition, costs can be attached to missed events or non-events.[4]

7.3 Logistic Regression

The linear regression methods described in Chapter 6 are not suitable for modeling time series of binary values. If the series is numerical but the outcome of interest is binary ("will next month's demand exceed 500 units?"), then we could potentially use linear regression to model the numerical series and then compare the numerical forecast to the threshold to create a binary forecast.

[4] For predictive measures and cost functions derived from the classification matrix, see the case in Section 9.3 and chapter Performance Evaluation in G. Shmueli, N. R. Patel, and P. C. Bruce. *Data Mining for Business Intelligence: Techniques, Concepts and Applications in Microsoft Office Excel with XLMiner*. John Wiley & Sons, 2nd edition, 2010

An popular alternative is to model the *probability* of the outcome of interest. In particular, a regression-type model suited for
modeling a binary y variable is *logistic regression*. Logistic regression is commonly used for predicting cross-sectional data. It is
less common in time series forecasting, perhaps because forecasting binary data is less common in general. When used with time
series, logistic regression can incorporate trend, seasonality, lag
variables, and external information. In a 2010 forecasting contest
of stock price movements (up/down), logistic regression was the
main tool used by the first and second place winners.[5]

In this section, we briefly introduce logistic regression and
then consider it in the time series context.[6]

In logistic regression, we model the relationship between the
odds of the event of interest and the predictors. *Odds* is a term
used in horse races and in betting in general. The relationship
between the odds of an event and the probability of an event is
$odds = \frac{p}{1-p}$, or equivalently $p = \frac{odds}{1+odds}$. For example, *odds*=2 (or
2:1) means that the event of interest is twice more likely to occur
than not to occur. *Odds*=2 correspond to $p = 2/3$.

For predictors $x_1, x_2, \ldots, x_p$, the logistic regression model is
given by

$$\log(odds) = \beta_0 + \beta_1 x_1 + \ldots + \beta_p x_p. \tag{7.3}$$

Hence, it is a multiplicative relationship between the odds and
the predictors. The function $\log(odds) = \log\left(\frac{p}{1-p}\right)$ is known as
the *logit* function in p. Note that as in linear regression:

- logistic regression is a model-based forecasting method (with
  all the implied advantages and weaknesses),

- the model can include different types of predictors (numerical,
  dummies, interactions, etc.), including seasonal dummies,
  trend terms (such as t), and lagged variables (such as y_{t-1}),

- all predictors should be available at the time of prediction,

- variable selection methods (such as stepwise, forward selection and backward elimination) can be used.

[5] For details and data on
the 2010 INFORMS stock
price movement forecasting
contest see the case in
Section 9.3.

[6] For a detailed description
of logistic regression in the
context of cross-sectional
prediction, see the chapter
on Logistic Regression in

G. Shmueli, N. R. Patel,
and P. C. Bruce. *Data Mining
for Business Intelligence:
Techniques, Concepts and
Applications in Microsoft
Office Excel with XLMiner.*
John Wiley & Sons, 2nd
edition, 2010

Lagged Predictors (y_{t-k})

When the binary data are the result of thresholding a continuous measurement (e.g., a thresholded blood sugar count), consider including lagged versions of the *actual measurements* rather than the binary values. For example, include the previous blood sugar count itself rather than whether it exceeded the threshold. Past actual measurements might be more predictive, assuming that they are available at the time of prediction.

Generating Binary Forecasts

Once we estimate the model in equation (7.3), we can obtain the predicted probability or predicted odds for each time period of interest. A binary forecast (event/non-event) is obtained by comparing the predicted probability to 0.5, or equivalently, by comparing the predicted odds to 1. A higher value leads to an "event" forecast, while a lower value leads to a "non-event" forecast.[7]

[7] Choosing a different probability or odds threshold can sometimes improve predictive performance.

Example: Rainfall in Melbourne, Australia

To illustrate the use of logistic regression for forecasting, consider the example of forecasting rainy days (yes/no) in Melbourne, Australia[8]. Data on daily rainfall amounts in Melbourne are publicly available at `www.bom.gov.au/climate/data`. We use data on rainfall between Jan 1, 2000 and Oct 31, 2011 (available in *MelbourneRainfall.xls*). The series includes the daily rainfall amount (in mm), as reported by the Melbourne Regional Office station (station number 086071).

We start by partitioning the series: here we use years 2000-2009 as the training period and years 2010-2011 as the validation period.[9] Next, we explore the series. Time plots of the binary daily data are not very informative, and hence we look at aggregated plots. Figure 7.1 shows a monthly aggregated time plot, which displays annual seasonality. Each line corresponds to a particular year, and a polynomial trend fitted to the monthly data highlights the annual seasonal pattern. We therefore model annual seasonality by including sine and cosine terms.

[8] Many thanks to Rob J Hyndman for pointing me to the data source and his paper (which inspired this example)

R. J. Hyndman. Nonparametric additive regression models for binary time series. In *Proceedings of the Australasian Meeting of the Econometric Society*, 1999

[9] This partitioning is useful for evaluating predictive performance of up to two years ahead.

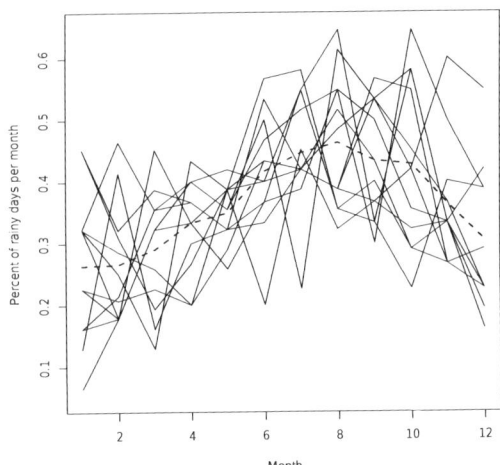

Figure 7.1: Percent of rainy days per month in Melbourne, Australia. Lines correspond to different years. Dotted line corresponds to the monthly averages.

We also include a lag-1 predictor to capture day-to-day rainfall correlation. For the lag variable, we can either include actual rainfall amount, or rain/no-rain. While both options should be considered, we display the results for using a lag-1 rainfall dummy predictor. Our model is therefore:

$$\log(odds(Rain)_t) = \beta_0 + \beta_1 Rain_{t-1} + \beta_2 \sin(2\pi t/365.25) + \beta_3 \cos(2\pi t/365.25)$$
$$(7.4)$$

A sample of the data, after creating the derived variables[10], is shown in Figure 7.2.

In R, we run a logistic regression using the function glm with family = "binomial". The resulting model and its predictive performance are shown in Tables 7.2 and 7.3, respectively. The classification matrix (also known as a confusion matrix in R's caret package) for the validation period shows a predictive accuracy of 64%, or error rate of 36%. In particular, the model predicts no-rainfall days with 94.7% accuracy (sensitivity) and rainfall days with 20% accuracy (specificity). Because the training period contains 36% of rainy days, a naive majority-class forecast of "no rain" on every day would have an identical 35% error rate. Hence, the logistic regression does not outperform this naive benchmark.

[10] A derived variable is a transformation of the original variables. In this case, sin, cos and $Rain_{t-1}$ are derived variables.

Date	Rainfall amount (millimetres)	Rainfall lag-1	Rain?	Lag1	t	Seasonal_sine	Seasonal_cosine
1/1/2000	0.4	1.8	1	1	1	0.017201575	0.999852042
1/2/2000	0	0.4	0	1	2	0.034398061	0.999408212
1/3/2000	0	0	0	0	3	0.051584367	0.99866864
1/4/2000	3.4	0	1	0	4	0.068755408	0.997633547
1/5/2000	1.4	3.4	1	1	5	0.085906104	0.996303238
1/6/2000	0	1.4	0	1	6	0.103031379	0.994678106
1/7/2000	0	0	0	0	7	0.120126165	0.992758634
1/8/2000	0	0	0	0	8	0.137185404	0.990545388
1/9/2000	0	0	0	0	9	0.154204048	0.988039023
1/10/2000	2.2	0	1	0	10	0.17117706	0.985240283
1/11/2000	0	2.2	0	1	11	0.188099418	0.982149993
1/12/2000	0	0	0	0	12	0.204966114	0.97876907
1/13/2000	0	0	0	0	13	0.221772158	0.975098513
1/14/2000	0	0	0	0	14	0.238512575	0.971139409
1/15/2000	0	0	0	0	15	0.255182413	0.966892929
1/16/2000	0.4	0	1	0	16	0.271776738	0.96236033
1/17/2000	0.8	0.4	1	1	17	0.288290641	0.957542953
1/18/2000	0	0.8	0	1	18	0.304719233	0.952442223
1/19/2000	0	0	0	0	19	0.321057654	0.947059651
1/20/2000	0	0	0	0	20	0.337301069	0.941396829

Figure 7.2: Sample of the rainfall dataset after creating the derived predictors. "Rain?" is the binary variable to be forecast.

Table 7.2: Summary of logistic regression model output.

```
> summary(rainy.lr)

Call:
glm(formula = Rainy ~ Lag1 + Seasonal_sine + Seasonal_cosine,
    family = "binomial", data = train.df)

Coefficients:
                Estimate Std. Error z value Pr(>|z|)
(Intercept)     -0.76888    0.03858 -19.927  < 2e-16 ***
Lag1             0.11187    0.01137   9.843  < 2e-16 ***
Seasonal_sine   -0.26885    0.05049  -5.324 1.01e-07 ***
Seasonal_cosine -0.37134    0.05067  -7.328 2.33e-13 ***
---
Signif. codes:  0 *** 0.001 ** 0.01 * 0.05 . 0.1   1
```

Table 7.3: Summary of logistic regression's predictive performance in the training and validation periods.

```
> confusionMatrix(ifelse(rainy.lr$fitted > 0.5, 1, 0), train.df$Rainy)

          Reference
Prediction   0    1          Accuracy : 0.6662
        0 2251 1115           Sensitivity : 0.9558
        1  104  182           Specificity : 0.1403


> confusionMatrix(ifelse(rainy.lr.pred > 0.5, 1, 0), valid.df$Rainy)

          Reference
Prediction   0    1          Accuracy : 0.6398
        0  373 220           Sensitivity : 0.9467
        1   21  55           Specificity : 0.2000
```

 code for creating Tables 7.2 and 7.3

```
library("caret")

rain.df <- read.csv("MelbourneRainfall.csv")
rain.df$Date <- as.Date(rain.df$Date, format="%m/%d/%Y")
rain.df$Rainy <- ifelse(rain.df$Rainfall > 0, 1, 0)
nPeriods <- length(rain.df$Rainy)
rain.df$Lag1 <- c(NA,rain.df$Rainfall[1:(nPeriods-1)])
rain.df$t <- seq(1, nPeriods, 1)
rain.df$Seasonal_sine = sin(2 * pi * rain.df$t / 365.25)
rain.df$Seasonal_cosine = cos(2 * pi * rain.df$t / 365.25)
train.df <- rain.df[rain.df$Date <= as.Date("12/31/2009", format="%m/%d/%Y"), ]
train.df <- train.df[-1,]
valid.df <- rain.df[rain.df$Date > as.Date("12/31/2009", format="%m/%d/%Y"), ]
xvalid <- valid.df[, c(4,6,7)]

rainy.lr <- glm(Rainy ~ Lag1 + Seasonal_sine + Seasonal_cosine, data = train.df, family = "binomial")
summary(rainy.lr)
rainy.lr.pred <- predict(rainy.lr, xvalid, type = "response")
confusionMatrix(ifelse(rainy.lr$fitted > 0.5, 1, 0), train.df$Rainy)
confusionMatrix(ifelse(rainy.lr.pred > 0.5, 1, 0), valid.df$Rainy)
```

Creating binary forecasts from predicted probabilities

To convert a forecasted probability into a binary forecast ("will the stock move up (1) or down (0)?"), we must choose a *cutoff value* or threshold on the probability. If the probability exceeds the cutoff, the prediction is "1". Otherwise it is "0". A popular default cutoff value is 0.5. In other words, if the "1" event is more likely (probability$>$0.5), we assign a "1" label. If the "1" event is less likely (probability$\leq$0.5), we assign a "0" label. Notice that in the R code for generating a confusion matrix in Table 7.3, we used a cutoff of 0.5 to classify the event of rain ("1") or no rain ("0").

7.4   Neural Networks

Among artificial intelligence algorithms used for predicting cross-sectional data, *neural networks* (also known as *artificial neural networks* or *neural nets*) are commonly used for time series forecasting, especially in financial forecasting, and when external information is useful. Neural networks can be used to generate numerical as well as binary forecasts.

The neural network algorithm is based on a model of biological activity in the brain, where neurons are interconnected and learn from experience. Neural nets are highly data-driven, and can become computationally expensive. Their structure supports capturing complex relationships between predictors and a response, and setting them up requires little user input. The "price" is that neural nets are considered a blackbox, in the sense that the relationship that they capture is not easy to understand. Hence, neural nets are good candidates for automated predictive tasks, where the main goal is generating accurate forecasts, but inadequate for descriptive or explanatory tasks.

In terms of performance, the forecasting literature includes inconclusive evidence regarding the performance of neural networks for time series forecasting. In tourism forecasting, for instance, neural networks were found to outperform other methods in a few cases while in others their performance was found to be inferior.[11] Similar results are reported in financial series

[11] C. J. Lin, H. F. Chen, and T. S. Lee. Forecasting tourism demand using time series, artificial neural networks and multivariate adaptive regression splines: Evidence from Taiwan. *International Journal of Business Administration*, 2(2):14–24, 2011

and renewable energy forecasting. It appears that the performance of neural networks is more beneficial with high frequency series, such as hourly, daily or weekly data, compared to low frequency series.[12] And finally, it can be combined with other methods to produce ensemble forecasts.

In this section we give a brief overview of neural nets and focus on their use for time series forecasting.[13]

The Neural Network Model

We have seen that linear regression can be used for modeling non-linear relationships between the predictors and the outcome variable by using transformations such as $\log(y)$ or creating *derived variables* from the predictor variables such as t^2 or $\sin(\pi t/365.25)$. Neural networks offer a further extension of linear regression, by creating *multiple layers of derived variables*.[14]

A neural network links the predictors and the outcome through a sequence of *layers*. In each layer, some operation is performed on the input information to produce an output (thereby creating a derived variable). The output of one layer is the input into the next layer. A neural network consists of three types of "layers", as illustrated in Figure 7.3:

1. An *input layer* accepts the input values of the predictors (numerical or binary)

2. One or more *hidden layers* create derived variables. A hidden layer receives inputs from the previous layer, performs some calculation on those inputs, and generates an output.

3. An *output layer* receives inputs from the last hidden layer and produces predicted values (numerical or binary).

Each layer contains *nodes*, denoted by circles in Figure 7.3. A node is a variable. The input layer nodes are the original predictor variables. For example, in Figure 7.3 nodes #1 and #2 take as input the values of predictors x_1 and x_2, respectively. Their output is identical to their input.

Hidden layer nodes are derived variables. In particular, they are a *weighted sum of the inputs* to which some monotone function, called an *activation function*, is applied. Common functions

[12] A performance comparison of neural nets to alternatives is given on the 2008 *NN5 Forecasting Competition for Neural Networks & Computational Intelligence* website neural-forecasting-competition.com/NN5/motivation.htm.

[13] On neural nets in cross-sectional prediction, see chapter "Neural Nets" in

G. Shmueli, N. R. Patel, and P. C. Bruce. *Data Mining for Business Intelligence: Techniques, Concepts and Applications in Microsoft Office Excel with XLMiner.* John Wiley & Sons, 2nd edition, 2010

[14] A derived variable is a transformation of the original variables. Examples include dummy variables created from a categorical variable and transformations such as $\log(y)$.

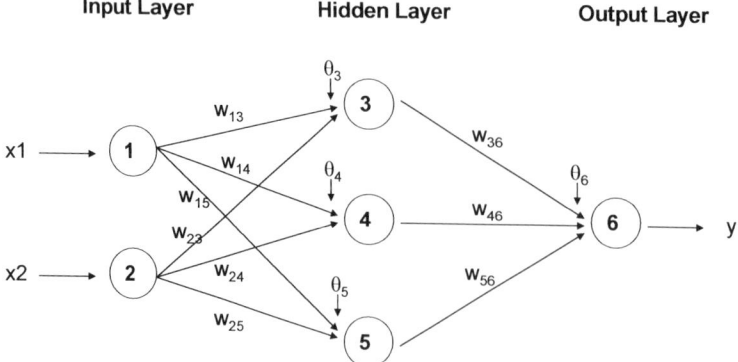

Figure 7.3: Schematic of a neural network with a single hidden layer, for predicting a single outcome (y) from two predictors (x_1, x_2)

are linear, exponential, and s-shaped functions such as the logit and hyperbolic tangent.[15].

[15] s-shaped or *sigmoidal* functions are common because of their squashing effect on very small and very large values while maintaining near-linearity for mid-range values. The two most common s-shaped functions are the *logit* function $g(s) = \frac{1}{1+\exp(-s)}$ and the *hyperbolic tangent* function $g(s) = -1 + \frac{2}{1+\exp(-s)}$

Node computation in technical terms

For a set of input values $x_1, x_2, \ldots, x_p$, the output of node j is the weighted sum $\theta_j \;\; + \;\; \sum_{i=1}^{p} w_{ij} x_i$, where $\theta_j, w_{1j}, \ldots, w_{pj}$ are weights that are initially set randomly and then adjusted as the network "learns". The constant θ_j controls the level of contribution of node j.

An activation function of choice ($g(s)$) is then applied to the weighted sum to produce the derived variable $g(\theta_j + \sum_{i=1}^{p} w_{ij} x_i)$, which is the output of node j.

In Figure 7.3, for instance, node #3 computes the weighted sum of nodes #1 and #2 as $\theta_3 + w_{13} x_1 + w_{23} x_2$. An activation function is then applied to this weighted sum. Similarly, the output node #6 is given by the activation function applied to a weighted sum of nodes #3, #4, and #5.

Linear regression, logistic regression and autoregressive models can be written as neural networks that lack hidden layers. This is important to notice, because in practice the best performing neural network is often the simplest one, that is, one with no hidden layers.[16] Figure 7.4 displays a neural network diagram for a linear or logistic regression with three predictors: a linear trend and two dummies for capturing an additive weekday/Saturday/Sunday seasonality pattern. Note that:

[16] N. K. Ahmed, A. F. Atiya, N. El Gayar, and H. El-Shishiny. An empirical comparison of machine learning models for time series forecasting. *Econometric Reviews*, 29:594–621, 2010

- a linear activation function corresponds to the linear regression model

$$y_t = \beta_0 + \beta_1 t + \beta_2 Weekday + \beta_3 Saturday + \epsilon$$

- an exponential activation function ($g(s) = \exp(s)$) corresponds to the linear regression model

$$\log(y_t) = \beta_0 + \beta_1 t + \beta_2 Weekday + \beta_3 Saturday + \epsilon$$

- a logit activation function corresponds to the logistic regression model

$$\log(odds)_t = \beta_0 + \beta_1 t + \beta_2 Weekday + \beta_3 Saturday$$

Figure 7.5 shows a neural network schematic for an AR(3) model (using a linear activation function).

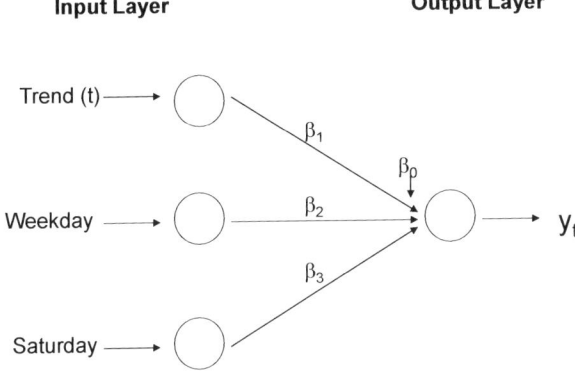

Figure 7.4: Schematic of a neural network reflecting a linear or logistic regression model with trend and weekday/Saturday/Sunday seasonality

A general schematic for a neural network used for forecasting a time series is shown in Figure 7.6. Note that a neural net can include multiple output nodes. In the context of time series forecasting, we use this to produce forecasts of different horizons. The schematic in Figure 7.6 is based on roll-forward forecasting, where forecasts for times $t + 1, t + 2, \ldots$ are based on the series "moving forward" one period at a time.   Additional hidden layers can be added in Figure 7.6 to further increase the complexity of the relationship between the inputs and output. The diagram can also be expanded to include external information by

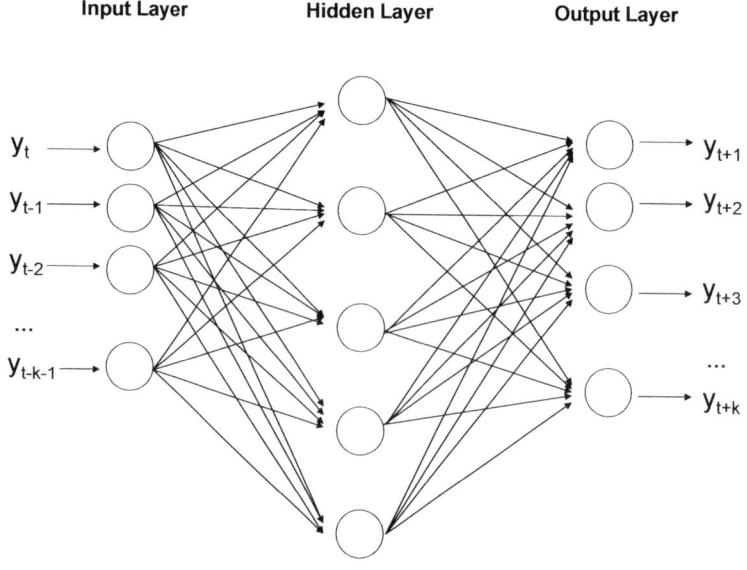

Input Layer

Output Layer

y_{t-1} ⟶ ◯

β_1

β_0

y_{t-2} ⟶ ◯ β_2 ⟶ ◯ ⟶ y_t

β_3

y_{t-3} ⟶ ◯

Figure 7.5: Schematic of a neural network reflecting an AR(3) model (assuming a linear activation function)

Input Layer

Hidden Layer

Output Layer

y_t ⟶

y_{t-1} ⟶

y_{t-2} ⟶

...

y_{t-k-1} ⟶

⟶ y_{t+1}

⟶ y_{t+2}

⟶ y_{t+3}

...

⟶ y_{t+k}

Figure 7.6: Schematic of a neural network reflecting a linear regression model with trend and week-day/Saturday/Sunday seasonality (assuming a linear activation function) specifying additional input nodes. In fact, successful applications of neural networks for time series forecasting are often based on including external information rather than extrapolation. For example, Law and Au[17] found that for forecasting annual Japanese tourist arrivals in Hong Kong, a neural network outperformed naive forecasts, linear regression, moving average, and exponential smoothing. The input layer of their neural network model included six nodes: Service Price, Average Hotel Rate, Foreign Exchange Rate, Population, Marketing Expenses, and Gross Domestic Expenditure. All of these capture external information.

[17] R. Law and N. Au. A neural network model to forecast Japanese demand for travel to Hong Kong. *Tourism Management*, 20:89–97, 1999

Pre-Processing

Three pre-processing issues should be considered prior to running a neural network:

Creating Derived Predictors: As in regression models, we can create predictors such as lagged versions of the time series, lagged versions of external information, seasonal dummies, and a time index to capture trend. These are then used as inputs to the neural network. In R, a neural network with generic predictors can be run using the avNNet function in the caret package. When the predictors are lagged versions of the time series, however, working with this function can be tedious. Fortunately, the forecast package offers a function that does all this work for us. The function is called nnetar, which stands for neural network autoregression. Throughout the rest of this chapter, we will focus on neural network autoregressions. To learn more about how to fit neural networks with generic predictors using avNNet in R, see Chapter 9 of the online textbook *Forecasting: Principles and Practice* by Hyndman and Athanasopoulos at www.otexts.org/fpp/9.

Removing rows with missing values: When creating lagged variables that will be included as predictors, rows with missing values must be removed. Again, in R, nnetar will do this work for you.

Scaling: Neural networks perform best when the predictors and response are on a scale of [0,1] or [-1,1]. Hence, in the time series context, the series itself as well as all predictors should be scaled before running the neural network. In R, the forecast package's nnetar function automatically scales the variables. When the predictors are lagged versions of the time series, scaling to [-1,1] is achieved by dividing by the maximum of the absolute values of the time series.

Removing trend and seasonality: There have been mixed reports in the literature regarding the need for removing trend and seasonality prior to using neural networks for forecasting time series. While some researchers claim that neural networks can automatically account for trend and seasonal patterns, substantial empirical evidence has shown that deseasonal-ization and de-trending improve the performance of neural networks.[18] To deseasonlize and/or de-trend a series, use any of the methods described in previous chapters (regression, ex-ponential smoothing, etc.) with the exception of differencing, which has been shown to lead to inferior performance.[19]

User Input

To run a neural network, users must determine the number of input nodes, the number of hidden layers, the number of nodes per hidden layer, the activation function, and the number of output nodes. Let us examine each choice separately:

The number of input nodes is equal to the number of predictors and is therefore problem-dependent. Generally, the more input nodes, the less time periods for the network to train on. Zhang and Kline conducted a large study on neural network forecasting and reached the conclusion that the number of predictors is a critical choice:

> [D]ifferent combinations of input variables can have significant impact on the model performance. Therefore, in applying [neural networks], it is critical to identify a set of important input variables to be included in the modeling process.

The number of hidden layers affects the level of complexity of the relationship between the inputs and outputs. Typically

[18] G. P. Zhang and D. M. Kline. Quarterly time-series forecasting with neural networks. *IEEE Transactions on Neural Networks*, 18(6):1800–1814, 2007

[19] N. K. Ahmed, A. F. Atiya, N. El Gayar, and H. El-Shishiny. An empirical comparison of machine learning models for time series forecasting. *Econometric Reviews*, 29:594–621, 2010

1-2 layers are sufficient. Using too many layers can cause overfitting, while too few lead to under-fitting.

The number of nodes per hidden layer requires trial and error. Using too few nodes will lead to under-fitting, while too many nodes will lead to overfitting. Comparing the training and validation performance can help in determining an adequate number.

Choice of activation function: The most common activation functions are s-shaped functions.

The number of output nodes depends on the number of forecasts that we want to generate. Some software packages are limited to a single output node.

Forecasting with Neural Nets in R

In R, a generic neural network—a network with predictors of any kind—are typically run with the function avNNet from the caret package. The avNNet function actually fits several neural networks and averages their outputs in order to come up with a forecast. Consequently, avNNet produces an ensemble forecast.

When working with time series, the pre-processing work that avNNet requires can be somewhat tedious. First, you need to set up lagged versions of the series as predictors and normalize them to [0,1] or [-1,1]. Once you have fit the model in the training period, you need to set up the predictors for the validation period. Here is where it can get tricky. When you want to forecast more than one-step ahead, some of the predictors in validation period will need to be forecasted values. For instance, suppose you want to forecast two-months ahead in a validation period and you have included the last two months' values as predictors in the training period. Your predictors in the validation period for the two-steps-ahead forecast will then need to include the last value in the training period and the one-step ahead forecast.

Fortunately, there is a function in R that will do all this pre-processing work for you when working with a time series. The function nnetar, which stands for neural network autoregression model, automatically pre-processes your time series before calling the avNNet function to fit and average several neural networks. Note that nnetar applies to time series where the only predictors are lagged versions of the series itself. To include other predictors, such as seasonal dummies, in a neural network, you will want to use avNNet.

The function nnetar has four main arguments: repeats, p, P, and size. The argument repeats controls the number of neural networks fit; the default is 20. If not specified, nnetar chooses the number of non-seasonal lags p based on the best-fit AR(p) model. For instance, a neural network autoregression with $p = 2$ would include the lag 1 and lag 2 of the series as inputs. The number of seasonal lags P is set to 1 as its default. A seasonal lag is the last observed value from the same season. For example, with monthly data, a neural network autoregression with $p = 2$ and $P = 1$ would include lag 1, lag 2, and lag 12 of the series as inputs. Because the function nnetar will only fit a neural network with a single hidden layer, size refers to the number of nodes in the hidden layer. Its default setting is the number of inputs nodes plus one $(p + P + 1)$ divided by two (and rounded to the nearest integer). We denote a neural network autoregression model by NNAR(p,P,size).

R's nnetar uses the *logit* activation function to map the input value into the hidden node's value. To go from the hidden nodes' values to the output value, nnetar uses either *linear* or *logit* activation function. When the series takes values on a continuous range, you will want to use the *linear* activation function by setting linout = TRUE as an argument in nnetar. For series with binary outcomes (rain or not), you set linout = FALSE to use the *logit* activation function when going from the hidden nodes' values to the output value. Using the *logit* activation function in this last step will ensure the output is a probability.

Example: Forecasting Amtrak Ridership

To illustrate the use of neural networks for forecasting a time series, we return to the Amtrak ridership example, using `nnetar`. Suppose that we are interested again in producing one-month-ahead, two-month-ahead,...,36-month-ahead forecasts.

Preparing the Data: The annual seasonality that characterizes the monthly ridership series can be addressed in several ways in the neural network:

1. include 11 non-seasonal lags and 1 seasonal lag as predictors

2. include 11 dummy variables

3. deseasonalize the series using some method

While each avenue can be investigated, we illustrate the results for the first option, which is a common choice in neural network forecasting. As usual, we partition the data into training and validation periods, such that the last 36 months are the validation period. Note that there are 159 months in the ridership time series. After dropping the first 12 months due to the lag variables and the 36 months for the validation period, the training period contains 111 months of data.

Neural Network Output: The output from running a neural network autoregression for forecasting monthly ridership is shown in Figure 7.7. The code for creating this figure is given below it. The NNAR(11,1,7) fitted is a neural network with the last 12 months as predictors (11 from the non-seasonal lags and 1 from the seasonal lag) and 7 hidden nodes. Because each neural network's parameters are initialized randomly before they are optimized, we set our seed at 201 so that we can replicate our results. Otherwise, the neural networks would be different each time we run `nnetar`. The `summary` line in the code below will print out the weights in a neural network, which we do not show here. For instance, by changing the number inside the double brackets to 2, you can see the weights for the second of 20 fitted neural networks.

The training and validation performance measures can be compared to the exponential smoothing models in Chapter 5 . In terms of performance measures, the neural network results are inferior to the Holt-Winter's method (Figure 5.6 and Table 5.5) in both the training and validation periods. In the training period, the neural network autoregression has an RMSE of 66.5, compared to Holt-Winter's 56.9. The neural network autoregression is significantly worse in the validation period. Its RMSE is 170.5 versus Holt-Winter's 82.2. Visually we can notice that the neural network is not picking up on the amplitude of seasonality in the way that the exponential smoothing model does. Unfortunately, even when we let nnetar choose the optimal neural network autoregression (using the call nnetar(train.ts), we find that the RMSE in the validation period drops only slightly to 159.4.

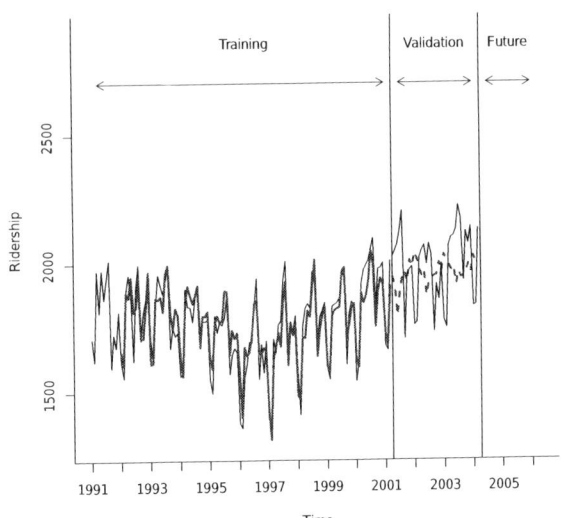

Figure 7.7: Neural network autoregression fitted to the Amtrak ridership data in the training period and forecasted in the validation period.

 code for creating Figure 7.7.

```
set.seed(201)
ridership.nnetar <- nnetar(train.ts, repeats = 20, p = 11, P = 1, size = 7)
summary(ridership.nnetar$model[[1]])
ridership.nnetar.pred <- forecast(ridership.nnetar, h = nValid)
accuracy(ridership.nnetar.pred, valid.ts)

plot(train.ts, ylim = c(1300, 2900),  ylab = "Ridership", xlab = "Time",
    bty = "l", xaxt = "n", xlim = c(1991,2006.25), lty = 1)
axis(1, at = seq(1991, 2006, 1), labels = format(seq(1991, 2006, 1)))
lines(ridership.nnetar.pred$fitted, lwd = 2, col = "blue")
lines(ridership.nnetar.pred$mean, lwd = 2, col = "blue", lty = 2)
lines(valid.ts)
```

7.5 Problems

1. For predicting whether the agricultural epidemic of *powdery mildew in mango* will erupt in a certain year in the state of Uttar Pradesh in India, Misra et al. (2004)[20] used annual outbreak records during 1987-2000. The epidemic typically occurs in the third and fourth week of March, and hence outbreak status is known by the end of March of a given year. The authors used a logistic regression model with two weather predictors (maximum temperature and relative humidity) to forecast an outbreak. The data are shown in the table below and are available in *PowderyMildewEpidemic.xls*.

[20] A. K. Misra, O. M. Prakash, and V. Rama-subramanian. Forewarning powdery mildew caused by Oidium mangiferae in mango (Mangifera indica) using logistic regression models. *Indian Journal of Agricultural Science*, 74(2):84–87, 2004

Year	Outbreak?	Max temperature	Relative humidity
1987	Yes	30.14	82.86
1988	No	30.66	79.57
1989	No	26.31	89.14
1990	Yes	28.43	91.00
1991	No	29.57	80.57
1992	Yes	31.25	67.82
1993	No	30.35	61.76
1994	Yes	30.71	81.14
1995	No	30.71	61.57
1996	Yes	33.07	59.76
1997	No	31.50	68.29
2000	No	29.50	79.14

Table 7.4: Data on Powdery Mildew in Mango outbreaks in Uttar Pradesh, India

(a) In order for the model to serve as a forewarning system for farmers, what requirements must be satisfied regarding data availability?

(b) Write an equation for the model fitted by the researchers in the form of equation (7.3). Use predictor names instead of x notation.

(c) Create a scatter plot of the two predictors, using different hue for epidemic and non-epidemic markers. Does there appear to be a relationship between epidemic status and the two predictors?

(d) Compute naive forecasts of epidemic status for years 1995-1997 using next-year forecasts ($F_{t+1} = F_t$). What is the naive forecast for year 2000? Summarize the results for these four years in a classification matrix.

(e) Partition the data into training and validation periods, so that years 1987-1994 are the training period. Fit a logistic regression to the training period using the two predictors, and report the outbreak probability as well as a forecast for year 1995 (use a threshold of 0.5).

(f) Generate outbreak forecasts for years 1996, 1997 and 2000 by repeatedly moving the training period forward. For example, to forecast year 1996, partition the data so that years 1987-1995 are the training period. Then fit the logistic regression model and use it to generate a forecast (use threshold 0.5).

(g) Summarize the logistic regression's predictive accuracy for these four years (1995-1997, 2000) in a classification matrix.

(h) Does the logistic regression outperform the naive forecasts?

(i) For year 1997, there is some uncertainty regarding the data quality of the outbreak status[21]. According to the logistic regression model, is it more likely that an outbreak occurred or not?

(j) If we fit a logistic regression with a lag-outbreak predictor such as $\log(odds)_t = \beta_0 + \beta_1 (Outbreak)_{t-1}$ to years 1987-1997, how can this model be used to forecast an outbreak in year 2000?

2. *Forecasting Australian Wine Sales:* Figure 6.31 shows time plots of monthly sales of six types of Australian wines (red, rose, sweet white, dry white, sparkling, and fortified) for 1980-1994. [Data available in *AustralianWines.xls*, source: Hyndman, R. J. Time Series Data Library, http://data.is/TSDLdemo; accessed on July 13, 2015.] The units are thousands of liters. You are hired to obtain short-term forecasts (1-12 months ahead) for each of the six series, and this task will be repeated every month.

[21] Different researchers report different outbreak status. See, for example https://goo.gl/qcq93e vs. the last page of https://goo.gl/9C4KKh

Figure 7.8: (Image by Naypong / FreeDigitalPhotos.net)

(a) Would you consider neural networks for this task? Explain why.

(b) Use neural networks to forecast fortified wine sales, as follows:

- Partition the data using the period until December 1993 as the training period.

- Run a neural network using R's nnetar with 11 non-seasonal lags (i.e., $p = 11$). Leave all other arguments at their default.

  i. Create a time plot for the actual and forecasted series over the training period. Create also a time plot of the forecast errors for the training period. Interpret what you see in the plots.

  ii. Use the neural network to forecast sales for each month in the validation period (January 1994 to December 1994).

(c) Compare your neural network to an exponential smoothing model used to forecast fortified wine sales.

  i. Use R's ets function to automatically select and fit an exponential smoothing model to the training period until December 1993. Which model did ets fit?

  ii. Use this exponential smoothing model to forecast sales for each month in 1994.

  iii. How does the neural network compare to the exponential smoothing model in terms of predictive performance in the training period? In the validation period?

8
Communication and Maintenance

8.1 Presenting Forecasts

Once a forecasting model is finalized and forecasts are produced, a critical step is presenting the forecasts to management or other stakeholders. Without proper presentation, the entire effort invested in the forecasting process can be lost. This section focuses on oral presentation, which is typically accompanied by slides. In Section 8.3 we discuss the presentation in written reports.

Proper presentation is audience-dependent. For managerial audiences it is better to avoid too much technical detail, and keep the focus on the forecasts, their uncertainty level, and various factors affecting them. For more technical audiences, one can include a high-level description of the forecasting method, the data used for generating forecasts, and the performance evaluation approach and results.

In what form should forecasts be presented? For presentation of the big picture and the forecasts in context, and especially for oral presentations, charts are a more appropriate choice than tables. For a single series, a time plot that includes both existing data and forecasts is commonly used. An example is shown in Figure 8.1, where the monthly series of search volume for the keywords "Business Analytics" on Google.com is displayed, alongside forecasts for the next 12 months (represented by a dashed line on a gray background). The choice of scale on the y-axis of the time plot should be carefully considered in light of the meaning of the units for the application. An overly-fine scale will magnify meaningless differences in values, while an overly-crude scale will mask meaningful differences.　　　If ex-

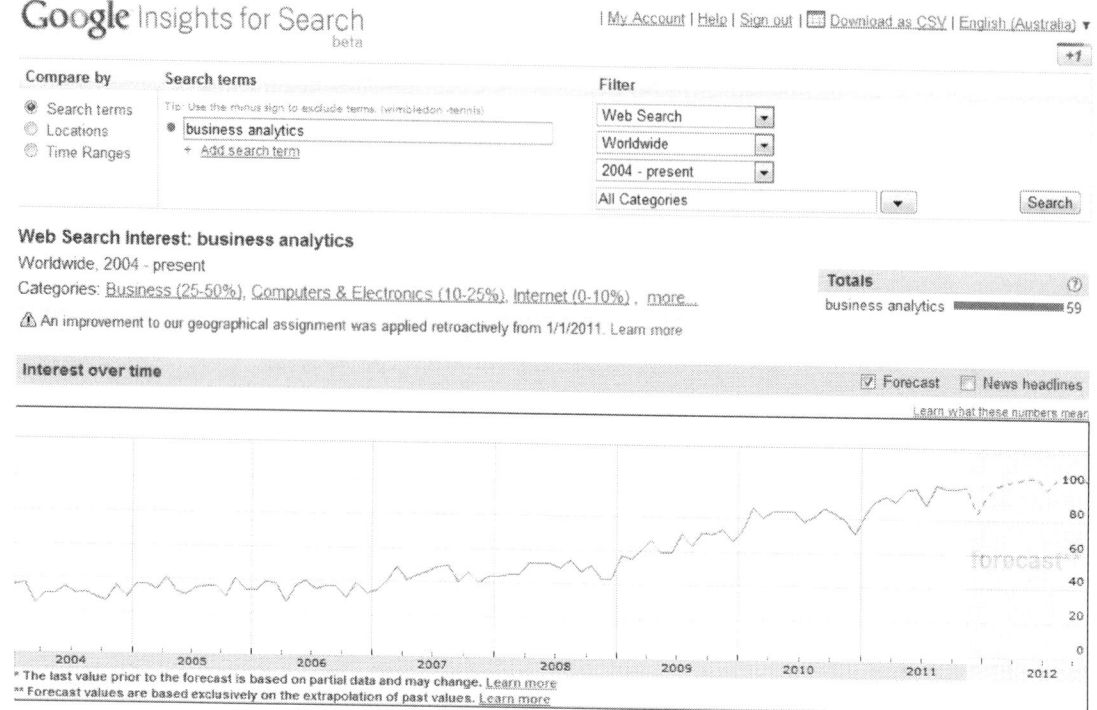

Figure 8.1: Time plot including forecasts for monthly search volume of keywords "Business Analytics" on Google.com

isting forecasting methods are being used or considered, the charts should include them as well, allowing an easy comparison with the new forecasting method. In cases where the presentation is aimed at choosing one forecasting method among a few alternatives (for reasons such as data or software availability, interpretability, or simplicity of application), the alternatives should be displayed on the same chart for ease of comparison. If only a few forecasted numbers are of interest, these numbers can be added to the chart using annotation.

　　Charts can also include intervals or shaded areas to display prediction intervals, as illustrated in Figure 8.2. In fact, displaying prediction intervals is highly desirable because forecasts are often perceived by users to be more certain than they really are.

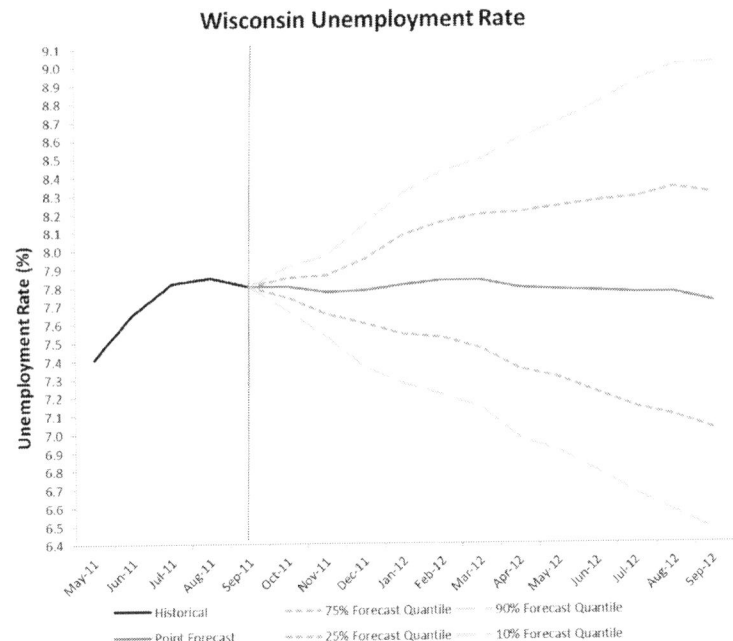

Figure 8.2: Presenting point forecasts and prediction intervals (Adapted from www.ssc.wisc.edu/~bhansen/forecast with permission from Bruce Hansen)

8.2   Monitoring Forecasts

When forecasts are generated on an ongoing basis it is imperative to occasionally re-assess performance. Extrapolation methods are based on the assumption that the conditions under which the forecasting takes place are identical to those occurring during the modeled period. However, conditions might change either gradually or drastically, thereby requiring the re-assessment of forecasts under the new conditions and perhaps even updating the forecasting method.

Monitoring forecasting performance can be achieved by plotting two charts: one displaying the actual and forecasted series and the other displaying the forecast errors. Although both charts are based on the same information, displaying the information from the two angles is complementary; it is easier to detect deterioration in forecast precision by examining the forecast error chart, while the actual/forecasted chart is more intuitive for grasping the direction of the deviations and their magnitude in the larger context.

Some experts advocate using *control charts*[1] for monitoring forecast errors. Control charts are time plots that also include lower and upper thresholds, as illustrated in Figure 8.3. If a threshold is exceeded, it is an indication that performance is "out of control" and action is needed. In the forecasting context, "out of control" means a change in the conditions affecting the series.

Standard control charts assume that the forecast error distribution is normal and stable over time. However, we have seen that the normality assumption is often violated (see Section 3.4). An alternative is to use the empirical distribution of forecast errors, as estimated from existing (past and present) data. The thresholds can be set, for example, as the 1st and 99th percentiles of the empirical distribution (see Section 3.4).

[1] For more information on control charts see the NIST/SEMATECH e-Handbook of Statistical Methods (itl.nist.gov/div898/handbook/pmc/section3/pmc31.htm)

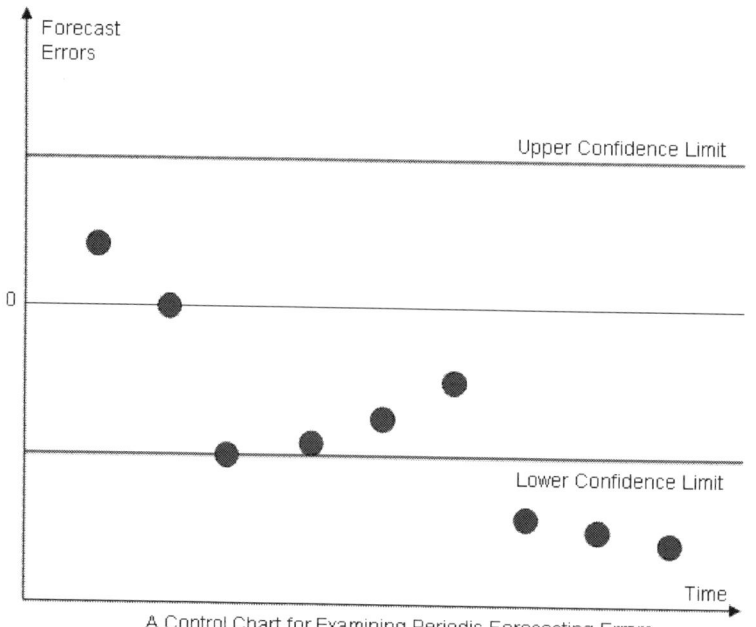

Figure 8.3: Control chart for monitoring forecast errors; Image from http://home.ubalt.edu/ntsbarsh/stat-data/forecast.htm, reproduced with permission from Hossein Arsham

8.3   Written Reports

Providing clear written reports about the forecasting process and the resulting forecasts is crucial for gaining the confidence of different stakeholders. The following two quotes illustrate the role of written documentation in light of skeptic audiences:

> "Forecasters should document exactly what they do. Even with very clear documentation, some skeptics will assume that the forecasters have fiddled with the numbers."[2]

> "Lack of understanding of NASS methodology and/or the belief in a hidden agenda can prevent market participants from correctly interpreting and utilizing the acreage and yield forecasts."[3]

[2] U.S. National Research Council. Forecasting demand and supply of doctoral scientists and engineers: Report of a workshop on methodology. National Academies Press, 2000

[3] See section 1.4

As in oral presentation, written reports of forecasting projects must cater to their audiences. An *executive summary* should include a high-level description of the problem, the data used, the method(s) used, the forecasts, and their expected precision. A time plot of the series and its forecasts is useful if the number of forecasted series is reasonably small. For a large number of series, a few examples can suffice along with a complete set of plots either in the appendix or in an online appendix. A *technical summary* can include further details about data processing (such as handling missing values), the motivation for choosing particular forecasting methods, the performance evaluation approach, and results from several approaches including benchmark models and any currently used methods.

Charts of the time series and their forecasts should be well formatted and easily readable. If the report is likely to be printed in black and white, it is better to use grayscale or other line differentiators in charts. For time plots, grayscale is typically preferable to different line types, as the human perception of continuity over time is lost with broken lines.

If the number of forecasted values is large, tables can supplement the charts for displaying the forecasted values. When reporting numerical forecasts, the level of rounding should be carefully considered. If the forecasts from the written report will be used as-is in practice, a sufficient number of decimals (depending on the problem at hand) should be supplied. If the reported numbers are only used for information, and the actual forecasts will be taken from an electronic source, then the level of rounding should be geared towards readability.

8.4 Keeping Records of Forecasts

When the forecasting task is an ongoing task, it is imperative to keep a record of forecasts and actual values, or equivalently, of forecasts and forecast errors. Such record keeping allows the evaluation of the forecasting method over time, its improvement when needed, and a comparison of the performance of the forecasting method with competing or alternative forecasting methods. Gathering sufficient forecast histories is also useful for quantifying the distribution of the forecast error, which can be used to generate predictive intervals. From a managerial point of view, records of forecasts and forecast errors provide "hard data" regarding performance that can be conveyed to stakeholders and used for planning as well as for obtaining a level of comfort with the forecasting method. In the next section we consider another important use of record keeping, related to imposed "forecast adjustments".

8.5 Addressing Managerial "Forecast Adjustment"

"Forecast Analyst" is a job title for an expert who produces forecasts for a company. Forecast analysts work in a wide variety of organizations and provide forecasts for various purposes. For example, a recent job posting for a "Senior Forecast Analyst" at Johnson & Johnson Consumer Companies, Inc.[4] included the following description:

[4] Job post available at www.ibf.com/bo/jnj.htm; accessed Dec 5, 2011

> The Senior Forecast Analyst is responsible for working with Marketing, Sales, and Operations to develop monthly and annual sales forecasts for J&J Consumer Company franchises. Specific responsibilities will include:
>
> - Influencing business decisions based on insight to market dynamics, category share, and the sales forecast.
> - Quantifying and influencing decisions on brand level risks and opportunities.

- Developing and updating complex forecasting models.
- Sharing insights and challenging assumptions at the monthly forecast meetings.
- Providing input to Sales & Marketing regarding predicted effectiveness of multiple promotional scenarios and their impact to the sales forecast.
- Identifying the drivers of variance in monthly forecasts.
- Analyzing data to quantify anticipated incremental sales from marketing events and new product launches.
- Composing and distributing monthly forecasting highlight reports.
- Developing sales forecast estimates for new products.
- Performing various ad hoc analyses and producing materials for senior level presentations.
- Representing the Forecasting department on cross-functional teams addressing new brand launches.
- Leading cross-company and cross-functional projects to create transformational improvement in forecast accuracy and process efficiency.

The inter-organizational role of a forecast analyst requires an understanding of how forecasts are used by different stakeholders and how those stakeholders are affected by the forecast values. In particular, a challenge to the successful implementation of forecasting into decision making is the widespread practice of "adjusting" forecasts by management or other decision makers in the organization.

One motivation for adjustment is specific agendas of different stakeholders, where costs or gains associated with over- or under-forecasting have different value to different stakeholders. An example is adjustments by different departments in the same organization. The marketing department might try to "adjust down" sales forecasts to emphasize the effectiveness of a new marketing strategy to be deployed, while the operations department might try to "adjust up" the same forecasts for inventory management purposes. Another example is adjustments by different levels of management: In an international pharmaceutical company, a country manager may want product sales forecasts to be as low as possible when bonuses are tied to exceeding that estimate, while a brand director at headquarters level may want as high a forecast as possible so as to secure the optimal level of resources for the product.[5]

Another motivation for forecast adjustment is knowledge of events that are not accounted for in the model. Research on whether such adjustments improve or degrade the final performance is inconclusive.

No matter the motivation behind the adjustments, a practical strategy is to keep a record of the forecasts before and after adjustment in order to accumulate objective data. Once actual data arrive, the information on forecasts and forecast errors should be reviewed to determine which approach is best. Obviously, "best" depends on the final goal of the forecasting task.

[5] "When forecasters take the floor: 6 tips on presenting a forecast" by Peter Mansell, blog post on eyeforpharma. com, Jun 28, 2011.

9
Cases

9.1 Forecasting Public Transportation Demand

Background

Forecasting transportation demand is important for multiple purposes such as staffing, planning, and inventory control. The public transport system in Santiago de Chile has gone through a major effort of reconstruction. In this context, a business intelligence competition took place in October 2006, which focused on forecasting demand for public transportation. This case is based on the competition, with some modifications.

Problem Description

A public transportation company is expecting increased demand for its services and is planning to acquire new buses and extend its terminals. These investments require a reliable forecast of future demand. To create such forecasts, one can use data on historic demand. The company's data warehouse has data on each 15-minute interval between 6:30 and 22:00, on the number of passengers arriving at the terminal. As a forecasting consultant, you have been asked to create a forecasting method that can generate forecasts for the number of passengers arriving at the terminal.

Figure 9.1: Vicente Valdes metro station, Santiago de Chile

Available Data

Part of the historic information is available in the file *bicup2006.xls*. The file contains the worksheet "Historic Information" with known demand for a 3-week period, separated into 15-minute intervals. The second worksheet ("Future") contains dates and times for a future 3-day period, for which forecasts should be generated (as part of the 2006 competition).

Assignment Goal

Your goal is to create a model/method that produces accurate forecasts. To evaluate your accuracy, partition the given historic data into two periods: a training period (the first two weeks) and a validation period (the last week). Models should be fitted only to the training data and evaluated on the validation data.

Although the competition winning criterion was the lowest Mean Absolute Error (MAE) on the future 3-day data, this is not the goal for this assignment. Instead, if we consider a more realistic business context, our goal is to create a model that generates reasonably good forecasts on any time/day of the week. Consider not only predictive metrics such as MAE, MAPE, and

RMSE, but also look at actual and forecasted values, overlaid on a time plot.

Assignment

For your final model, present the following summary:

1. Name of the method/combination of methods

2. A brief description of the method/combination

3. All estimated equations associated with constructing forecasts from this method

4. The MAPE and MAE for the training period and the validation period

5. Forecasts for the future period (March 22-24), in 15-min intervals

6. A single chart showing the fit of the final version of the model to the entire period (including training, validation, and future). Note that this model should be fitted using the combined training + validation data

Tips and Suggested Steps

1. Use exploratory analysis to identify the components of this time series. Is there a trend? Is there seasonality? If so, how many "seasons" are there? Are there any other visible patterns? Are the patterns global (the same throughout the series) or local?

2. Consider the frequency of the data from a practical and technical point of view. What are some options?

3. Compare the weekdays and weekends. How do they differ? Consider how these differences can be captured by different methods.

4. Examine the series for missing values or unusual values. Suggest solutions.

5. Based on the patterns that you found in the data, which models or methods should be considered?

6. Consider how to handle actual counts of zero within the computation of MAPE.

9.2 Forecasting Tourism (2010 Competition, Part I)

Background

Tourism is one of the most rapidly growing global industries and tourism forecasting is becoming an increasingly important activity in planning and managing the industry (from kaggle.com).

Problem Description

The 2010 tourism forecasting competition had two parts. In part I, competitors were tasked with producing forecasts for the next four years, given 518 series of annual tourism data.

Figure 9.2: (Image by winnond / FreeDigitalPhotos.net)

Available Data

The data consist of 518 annual series, each related to some (undisclosed) tourism activity. Tourism activities include inbound tourism numbers to one country from another country, visitor nights in a particular country, tourism expenditure, etc. The series differ in length, ranging from 7-year series to 43-year series. They also differ in the order of magnitude of values.

The data are available at www.kaggle.com/c/tourism1/Data (download the file "tourism_data.csv").[1]

[1] Downloading the data requires creating a free account on kaggle.com

Assignment Goals

This case will give you experience with forecasting a large number of series. While the competition goal was to achieve the highest predictive accuracy, the goal of this case is to highlight different aspects of the forecasting process that pertain to forecasting a large number of series. For example, easy-to-use visualization tools have a significant advantage for visualizing a large number of series.

Note that the multiple series in this case are not likely to be forecasted together. However, it is common to forecast the demand for a large number of series, such as products in a supermarket chain.

Another aspect of this case is the use of different predictive measures, and handling practical issues such as zero counts and summarizing forecast accuracy across series.

The assignment provides guidelines for walking you through the forecasting process. Remember that the purpose is not winning the (already completed) contest, but rather learning how to approach forecasting of a large number of series.

Assignment

1. Plot all the series (an advanced data visualization tool is recommended) - what type of components are visible? Are the series similar or different? Check for problems such as missing values and possible errors.

2. Partition the series into training and validation, so that the last 4 years are in the validation period for each series. What is the logic of such a partitioning? What is the disadvantage?

3. Generate naive forecasts for all series for the validation period. For each series, create forecasts with horizons of 1,2,3, and 4 years ahead ($F_{t+1}, F_{t+2}, F_{t+3}$, and F_{t+4}).

4. Which measures are suitable if we plan to combine the results for the 518 series? Consider MAE, Average error, MAPE and RMSE.

5. For each series, compute MAPE of the naive forecasts once for the training period and once for the validation period.

6. The performance measure used in the competition is *Mean Absolute Scaled Error* (MASE). Explain the advantage of MASE and compute the training and validation MASE for the naive forecasts.

7. Create a scatter plot of the MAPE pairs, with the training MAPE on the x-axis and the validation MAPE on the y-axis. Create a similar scatter plot for the MASE pairs. Now examine both plots. What do we learn? How does performance differ between the training and validation periods? How does performance range across series?

8. The competition winner, Lee Baker, used an ensemble of three methods:

- Naive forecasts multiplied by a constant trend (global/local trend: "globally tourism has grown "at a rate of 6% annually.")

- Linear regression

- Exponentially-weighted linear regression

(a) Write the exact formula used for generating the first method, in the form $F_{t+k} = \ldots (k = 1, 2, 3, 4)$

(b) What is the rational behind *multiplying* the naive forecasts by a constant? (Hint: think empirical and domain knowledge!)

(c) What should be the dependent variable and the predictors in a linear regression model for these data? Explain.

(d) Fit the linear regression model to the first five series and compute forecast errors for the validation period.

(e) Before choosing a linear regression, the winner described the following process

> "I examined fitting a polynomial line to the data and using the line to predict future values. I tried using first through fifth order polynomials to find that the lowest MASE was obtained using a first order polynomial (simple regression line). This best fit line was used to predict future values. I also kept the $[R^2]$ value of the fit for use in blending the results of the predictor."

What are two flaws in this approach?

(f) If we were to consider exponential smoothing, what particular type(s) of exponential smoothing are reasonable candidates?

(g) The winner concludes with possible improvements, one being "an investigation into how to come up with a blending [ensemble] method that doesn't use as much manual tweaking would also be of benefit". Can you suggest methods or an approach that would lead to easier automation of the ensemble step?

(h) The competition focused on minimizing the average MAPE of the next four values across all 518 series. How does this goal differ from goals encountered in practice when considering tourism demand? Which steps in the forecasting process would likely be different in a real-life tourism forecasting scenario?

Tips and Resources

The winner's description of his approach and experience: `blog.kaggle.com/2010/09/27/`

Article "The tourism forecasting competition", by Athanasopoulos, Hyndman, Song and Wu `robjhyndman.com/papers/forecompijf.pdf`, International Journal of Forecasting, April 2011.

9.3   Forecasting Stock Price Movements (2010 INFORMS Competition)

Background

Traders, analysts, investors and hedge funds are always looking for techniques to better predict stock price movements. Knowing whether a stock will increase or decrease allows traders to make better investment decisions. Moreover, good predictive models allow traders to better understand what drives stock prices, supporting better risk management (from kaggle.com).

Problem Description

The 2010 INFORMS Data Mining Contest challenged participants to generate accurate forecasts of 5-minute stock price movements (up/down) for a particular stock over a forecast horizon of 60 minutes.

Available Data

The data to be forecasted, named "TargetVariable", is a time series of intraday trading data, showing stock price movements at five minute intervals. Values of this series are binary (0/1) to reflect up/down movements in the next 60 minutes.

Additional external data include sectoral data, economic data, experts' predictions and indexes. These data are in the form of 609 time series named "Variable...". The first column in the file is the timestamp. The length of all series is 5922 periods.

The data are available at www.kaggle.com/c/informs2010/Data. Download the file "TrainingData.zip"[2] (the other file "Test-Data.zip" contains the template for submitting forecasts and is not needed for this case).

[2] Downloading the data requires creating a free account on kaggle.com

Assignment Goals

This assignment will give you experience with forecasting binary outcomes for high-frequency data and with integrating external data into a forecasting method. In particular, this task highlights the difficulty of searching for useful external information among a large number of potential external variables.

While the winning criterion in the competition was a particular predictive measure on a test set, the purpose of this case is not focused on achieving the highest predictive accuracy but rather to to come up with practical solutions that can then be implemented in practice. Another goal is to evaluate whether a series, in this case stock price movements, can be forecasted at better-than-random accuracy.

Assignment

1. Create a time plot of the target variable and of Variable74OPEN using temporal aggregation. Explore the data for patterns, extreme and missing values.

    (a) One participant reported that differencing the predictor variables at lag 12 was useful. Compare boxplots and histograms of Variable74OPEN by target variable to the same plots of the differenced Variable74OPEN by target variable.

    (b) Find the three dates when there were days with no data. What are solutions for dealing with these missing values?

    (c) Examine carefully the data at 3:55pm daily. Some competitors noticed that this period always had larger gains/losses, suspecting that it represents the start/end of a trading day, and therefore more than 5 minutes. This is an example where a competition differs from real life forecasting: in real life we would know exactly when the trading day starts and ends. How can this information help improve forecasts for these periods?

2. Partition the data into training and validation, so that the last 2539 periods are in the validation period. How many minutes does the validation period contain?

3. What is the percent of periods in the training period that have a value of 1?

4. Report the classification matrix for using majority-class forecasts on the validation period.

5. Generate naive forecasts for the validation period, using the most recent value. Report the classification matrix for the naive forecasts.

6. One of the top performing competitors used logistic regression, initially with Variable74 variables (high, low, open, and close) as predictors. In particular, he used lagging and differencing operations. To follow his steps, create 12-differenced predictors based on the Variable74 variables, and lag the target variable by 13 periods. The model should include the original Variable74 predictors and the differenced versions (eight predictors in total). Report the estimated regression model.

7. Use the logistic regression model to forecast the validation period. Report the classification matrix. How does the logistic model perform compared to the two benchmark forecast approaches?

8. The winning criterion in this contest was the highest *Area Under the Curve*[3] (AUC) averaged across the results database. Recall that most forecasting methods for binary outcomes generate an event *probability*. The probability is converted to a binary forecast by applying a threshold. The AUC measure is computed from the classification matrix by considering all possible probability thresholds between 0 and 1. Consider the following classification matrix, where $a, b, c,$ and d denote the counts in each cell:

[3] See also the evaluation page on the contest website www.kaggle.com/c/informs2010/Details/Evaluation

	predicted events	predicted non-events
actual events	a	b
actual non-events	c	d

The AUC is computed as follows:

- Obtain the classification matrix for a particular probability threshold (recall that the default is a threshold of 0.5).
- Compute the two measures *sensitivity*$= \frac{a}{a+b}$ and *specificity*$= \frac{d}{c+d}$.

- Repeat the last two steps for probability thresholds ranging from 0 to 1 in small steps (such as 0.01).

- Plot the pairs of *sensitivity* (on the y-axis) and *1-specificity* (x-axis) on a scatterplot, and connect the points. The result is a curve called an *ROC Curve*.

- The area under the ROC curve is called the *AUC*. Computing this area is typically done using an algorithm.

High AUC values indicate better performance, with 0.50 indicating random performance and 1 denoting perfect performance.

(a) Using the logistic regression model that you fitted in the last section, compute *sensitivity* and *1-specificity* on the validation period for the following thresholds: 0, 0.1, 0.2, 0.3, 0.4, 0.5, 0.6, 0.7, 0.8, 0.9, 1. This can be easily done by modifying the probability threshold on the Excel LR_Output worksheet.

(b) Create a scatter plot of the 11 pairs and connect them. This is the ROC curve for your model.

9. While AUC is a popular performance measure in competitions, it has been criticized for not being practically useful and even being flawed. In particular, Rice (2010) points out that in practice, a single probability threshold is typically used, rather than a range of thresholds. Other issues relate to lack of external validity and low precision. He suggests:[4]

> "[I]nstead of picking a model winner in what could be a random AUC lottery, apparently more accurate measures - straight classification error rate and average squared error - with much better statistical and external validity should probably now be considered."

Compute the classification error rate $\left(\frac{b+c}{a+b+c+d}\right)$ for the logistic regression model, using the validation period.

10. The same competitor, Christopher Hefele, then added more predictors to his model: Variable167 and Variable55 (each consisting of four series). His AUC was increased by 0.0005. Is this additional complexity warranted in practice? Fit a logistic regression with the additional predictors (taking appropriate

[4] D. M. Rice. Is the AUC the best measure?, September 2010. available at www.riceanalytics.com/_wsn/page15.html

differences), generate forecasts for the validation period, and compare the classification matrix and classification error rate to that of the simpler model (with Variable74 predictors only).

11. Use a neural network with the three sets of differenced and original variables (74, 167, and 55) as predictors. Generate forecasts and report the classification matrix and classification error rate. How does the neural network's performance compare to the two benchmark methods and the logistic regression model?

12. Which of the different models that you fitted would you recommend a stock trader use for forecasting stock movements on an ongoing basis? Explain.

Tips and Resources

- The top three performers' description of their approaches and experience: `blog.kaggle.com/2010/10/11/`

- Forum with postings by top performers and other contestants after the close of the contest: `www.kaggle.com/c/informs2010/forums/t/133/and-the-winner-is`

Data Resources, Competitions, and Coding Resources

To further assist readers and students with hands-on learning, below is a list of several publicly available, online sources of time series data that can be used for further study, projects, or otherwise.

Publicly Available Time Series Data

- Google Flu Trends - `www.google.org/flutrends`

- Time Series Data Library - `data.is/TSDLdemo`

- Financial Time Series - `finance.yahoo.com`

- Forecastingprinciples.com Website - `http://www.forecastingprinciples.com/index.php/data`

- US Census Bureau business and industry series - `www.census.gov/econ/currentdata/datasets/`

Forecasting Competitions

Engaging in a competition is another good and exciting way to learn more about forecasting. However, remember that competitions are "sanitized" environments, which lack the real challenges of determining the goal, cleaning the data, evaluating performance in a business-relevant way, and implementing the forecasting system in practice.

Many of the competitions listed below are annual, and open to anyone interested in competing. Some are recent one-time competitions. Some competition websites make data from past competitions available, including reports by the winners.

- The Time Series Forecasting Grand Competition for Computational Intelligence - `www.neural-forecasting-competition.com`

- The North American collegiate weather forecasting competition - `wxchallenge.com`

- Tourism Forecasting - `www.kaggle.com/c/tourism1` and `www.kaggle.com/c/tourism2`

- M-Competition - Links to the M4 and all past competitions in the series are available at `m4competition.com/links-past-competitions`

Coding Resources

To learn more about coding in R, the following resources may be helpful:

- *Google's R Style Guide* - `https://google-styleguide.googlecode.com/svn/trunk/Rguide.xml`

- *R For Dummies* by Andrie de Vries and Joris Meys

- *R Cookbook* by Paul Teetor

- *R for Everyone: Advanced Analytics and Graphics* by Jared P. Lander

- *R in a Nutshell* by Joseph Adler

- *A Beginner's Guide to R* by Alain Zuur, Elena Ieno, and Erik Meesters

- DataCamp's *Introduction to R* - `https://www.datacamp.com/courses/free-introduction-to-r`

- Leada's *R Bootcamp* - `https://www.teamleada.com/courses/r-bootcamp`

- Coursera's *Data Science Specialization* (9 course sequence) by Johns Hopkins University faculty - `https://www.coursera.org/specialization/jhudatascience/1`.

Bibliography

[1] N. K. Ahmed, A. F. Atiya, N. El Gayar, and H. El-Shishiny. An empirical comparison of machine learning models for time series forecasting. *Econometric Reviews*, 29:594–621, 2010.

[2] R. R. Andrawis, A. F. Atiya, and H. El-Shishiny. Forecast combinations of computational intelligence and linear models for the NN5 time series forecasting competition. *International Journal of Forecasting*, 27:672–688, 2011.

[3] S. Asur and B. A. Huberman. Predicting the future with social media. In *IEEE/WIC/ACM International Conference on Web Intelligence and Intelligent Agent Technology (WI-IAT)*, pages 492 – 499, 2010.

[4] R. Batchelor. Accuracy versus profitability. *Foresight: The International Journal of Applied Forecasting*, 21:10–15, 2011.

[5] BBC News Europe. Italy scientists on trial over L'aquilla earthquake, 2011. Accessed Nov 1, 2011.

[6] BBC News Science & Environment. Can we predict when and where quakes will strike?, 2011. Accessed Nov 1, 2011.

[7] R. M. Bell, Y. Koren, and C. Volinsky. All together now: A perspective on the Netflix Prize. *Chance*, 23:24–29, 2010.

[8] H. S. Burkom, S. P. Murphy, and G. Shmueli. Automated time series forecasting for biosurveillance. *Statistics in Medicine*, 26:4202–4218, 2007.

[9] C. Chatfield. *The Analysis of Time Series: An Introduction.* Chapman & Hall/CRC, 6th edition, 2003.

[10] E. J. Gardner. Exponential smoothing: The state of the art - Part II. *International Journal of Forecasting*, 22:637–666, 2006.

[11] R. J. Hyndman. Nonparametric additive regression models for binary time series. In *Proceedings of the Australasian Meeting of the Econometric Society*, 1999.

[12] R. J. Hyndman. Another look at forecast-accuracy metrics for intermittent demand. *Foresight: The International Journal of Applied Forecasting*, 4:43–46, 2006.

[13] R. Law and N. Au. A neural network model to forecast Japanese demand for travel to Hong Kong. *Tourism Management*, 20:89–97, 1999.

[14] C. J. Lin, H. F. Chen, and T. S. Lee. Forecasting tourism demand using time series, artificial neural networks and multivariate adaptive regression splines: Evidence from Taiwan. *International Journal of Business Administration*, 2(2):14–24, 2011.

[15] A. K. Misra, O. M. Prakash, and V. Ramasubramanian. Forewarning powdery mildew caused by Oidium mangiferae in mango (Mangifera indica) using logistic regression models. *Indian Journal of Agricultural Science*, 74(2):84–87, 2004.

[16] D. M. Rice. Is the AUC the best measure?, September 2010. available at www.riceanalytics.com/_wsn/page15.html.

[17] G. Shmueli, N. R. Patel, and P. C. Bruce. *Data Mining for Business Intelligence: Techniques, Concepts and Applications in Microsoft Office Excel with XLMiner.* John Wiley & Sons, 2nd edition, 2010.

[18] S. S. Soman, H. Zareipour, O. Malik, and P. Mandal. A review of wind power and wind speed forecasting methods with different time horizons. In *Proceedings of the 42nd North American Power Symposium (NAPS), Arlington, Texas, USA*, 2010.

[19] M. A. Tannura, S. H. Irwin, and D. L. Good.   Weather, technology, and corn and soybean yields in the U.S. corn belt. Marketing and Outlook Research Report 2008-01, Department of Agricultural and Consumer Economics, University of Illinois at Urbana-Champaign, 2008.

[20] J. W. Taylor. Exponentially weighted methods for forecasting intraday time series with multiple seasonal cycles. *International Journal of Forecasting*, 26:627–646, 2003.

[21] J. W. Taylor. Smooth transition exponential smoothing. *Journal of Forecasting*, 23:385–394, 2004.

[22] J. W. Taylor and R. D. Snyder. Forecasting intraday time series with multiple seasonal cycles using parsimonious seasonal exponential smoothing. *Omega*, forthcoming, 2011.

[23] U.S. National Research Council. Forecasting demand and supply of doctoral scientists and engineers: Report of a workshop on methodology. National Academies Press, 2000.

[24] G. P. Zhang and D. M. Kline. Quarterly time-series forecasting with neural networks. *IEEE Transactions on Neural Networks*, 18(6):1800–1814, 2007.

Index

12205914R00116

Printed in Great Britain
by Amazon.co.uk, Ltd.,
Marston Gate.